ONE TYRE FIRE: A TALE OF THE MAZDA-SEVENS

Introduction:

Hello and welcome. My name is Ayrton Rogers and for some reason, unbeknownst to me, I have decided to start writing a book. I have no idea why, I woke up an hour before my alarm was due to go off this morning, and for some reason thought, "why not - bollocks, let's write a book!"

The date is February the 4th, 2023, the day I was initially due to be picking up the chassis for my new car. However, due to unforeseen circumstances, it isn't ready for collection. The 2023 750 Motor Club Ma7da championship is due to start in 70 days, and I intend to be at the first meeting – how realistic that is, only time will tell.

This is a short story of my journey, a tale if you will. God knows if my writing is good enough to deem this as a tale or not, chances are that this will more than likely just become a diary for me to look back on in the years to come. Nonetheless, I hope you enjoy the stories to follow.

CONTENTS

One Tyre Fire: A Tale of the Mazda-Sevens

Chapter 1 – An Epiphany   1

Chapter 2 – 600 miles and 1 big decision   3

Chapter 3 – "Do you want to build a racecar?"   9

Chapter 4 – The end of an era   16

Chapter 5 – New Beginnings   19

Chapter 6 – Day 1, 61 Days until Croft   22

Chapter 7 – "It's looking a bit touch-and-go now."   26

Chapter 8 – "It's got fuel, it's got compression…"   30

Chapter 9 – The Secret Signal   35

Chapter 10 – Can I ask a favour?   45

Chapter 11 – "I'm pretty sure I nearly drowned out there!"   48

Chapter 12 – "Aaaaand breathe!"   68

Chapter 13 – Who'd've guessed, another long   73

journey!

Chapter 14 – Upgrades people, upgrades!	87
Chapter 15 – "Well damn, wasn't expecting that!"	90
Chapter 16 – "Ummm, what do we do now?"	103
Chapter 17 – "Are you feeling ok?"	106
Chapter 18 – Happy Birthday Mum!	122
Chapter 19 – Time to get back to business.	127
Chapter 20 – 400 miles, 18 hours and 2 races	130
Chapter 21 – So, what was going wrong?	143
Chapter 22 – 3-cheers for early starts! Hip-hip…	150
Chapter 23 – The final chapter (figuratively, there are more chapters after this one)	155
Chapter 24 – "Well, what now then…"	168
Acknowledgements	169

CHAPTER 1 – AN EPIPHANY

Date: Somewhere mid 2022

Time: Late at night

Location: The Garage

As Dad and I are down the garage for another long and tiring night getting the Mallock ready for the next meeting, working frantically on the complicated and overly constrained design (who's dumb idea was it to shoehorn a Vauxhall C20XE "Red Top" into a Mallock Mk27 anyway!.....Oh wait, that was my dumb idea!), the question is asked; "Why don't we just sell up everything and buy a couple of cars that are simple, don't need much work, and cheap, so we can get back to enjoying our racing again?". Honestly, in my state of only a few hours' sleep, nothing but Monster and Coffee pulsing through my veins, and the odd Oreo for sustenance, that sounded like the best idea I had ever heard!

The thought had crossed my mind numerous

times before, but this time hit harder. The Mallock came into my hands in late 2017, and had been built by myself, friends, and family members until it was first raced in 2020. After coming together with the wall at Oulton Park at the end of the season, the car was completely redesigned and engineered to what it was today. An ungodly number of hours (and I'm not even going to comprehend how much money) went into the car, and I was really hoping that it was going to pay dividends. That weekend was the second meeting of the year for me in the Mallock at Brands Hatch with the Clubmans Sports Prototypes, and as much as I was excited, I couldn't help but think about the prospect of something simpler and cheaper. From reading the regulations of the Ma7da class, I could almost tell that my mind was made up! No matter, I gave myself the meeting to come to a decision on my own.

Fast forward to Sunday afternoon when the Mallock is being hiab'ed onto the back of the trailer because *someone* got a little too excited, on what turned out to be too cold tyres, and put the car front end into the barrier at Surtees – at least I was right in front of the Medical Centre for the obligatory check up! After we had been fighting with reliability in the car all weekend already, I needed no further convincing, and the Era of Mallock for Team Rogers Racing was at an end.

CHAPTER 2 – 600 MILES AND 1 BIG DECISION

Date: Sunday 2nd October, 2022

Time: 05:00

Location: My house

Following the incident at Brands Hatch, the Mallock was put up for sale, and myself and my good buddy, Ross Loram, jumped into my trusty ol' Civic (brilliantly dubbed Clifford the Big Red Dog when I bought him many, many years ago) for the 6-hour journey up to Snetterton Circuit in Norfolk, for the final meeting of the season in the Ma7da Championship.

I was at a friends wedding the night before this journey, and was deemed absolutely crazy to drive halfway across the country just to watch some racing. However, when you are based down in Devon, you quickly come to understand that if you want to go racing, everywhere is bloody miles away! Even Thruxton or Castle Combe (which are our "locals") are the best part of 2 hours away. Brands, Pembrey, Mallory – 3 hours on a good run. But Ross and I needed to see what the fuss was about, by this point in time, I had (somehow) managed to convince him that he needed to dust off the old helmet (no, not a euphemism!) and get back out there. The prospect of the Ma7da championship was something that both of us were extremely excited with – we'd watched all of the races on YouTube, read and re-read the regulations god knows how many times, researched all of the parts, details and specifics about the championship to the finest details! We knew that this was the championship for us!

We've both spent our lives in and around racing. Ross and his dad, Brian, have been heavily involved in short circuit oval racing, continuing this theme onto the big circuits in the form of their Silhouette spec Vauxhall Tigra A. I never got behind the wheel of a short circuit machine, but my dad, Lee Rogers, spent his youth in Bangers, Hot Rods, and Stock Rods before moving into the Pickup Truck Racing Championship – which aside from the Silhouettes, is the natural stepping stone for short circuit drivers to make the leap onto the big ones. Unfortunately, as I was 7 when Dad started in the Pickups, I would have been a little too short to reach the pedals!

However, since I learned to drive, I have managed my way onto the track a couple of times, building and racing a Citroen AX Classic Touring Car when I was 20, and then the Mallock as I have explained already. Ma7da, with its lightweight seven-esque construction, MX5 1800 engine and gearbox and rear wheel drive seemed to be a good stepping stone.

We pulled into Snetterton at exactly 10am – the early morning lack of traffic had done us a treat and we'd managed to make what is normally a roughly 6-hour drive, exactly 5 hours long (with no speeding might I just add!). We didn't really know what to expect when we saw these cars, and were hoping that we could meet a couple of drivers, team members and crew and start to get a more rounded idea of what was ahead of us. The Ma7da paddock was against the start/finish straight and closest to the holding area so as you walk into the paddock from the car park, these cars were very prominently located. Unfortunately for us, the early October weather was not on our side, and although there was no rain, the wind was cold and spiteful, despite the blue skies and sun shining – go figure! But because of this, there were no drivers or crew anywhere to be seen. "No matter", we thought, "we'll have a wander up and down, and we will surely find someone, somewhere whose brain we can pick". So, we wandered up and down the paddock, getting a good look at all the cars; if I recall correctly, it was after seeing the very first one that we both went "These things are epic! I want one".

Race 1 came about, and Ross and I took refuge on the big mound at Agostini so we could get a good view of the track. As the cars first came into view, hurtling down to the hairpin we were stood, 4 wide we couldn't help but think "there is no way they are all going to make it through there!", but somehow, and with no doubt a lot of assistance of that special added bit with racing – luck, they all made it through and continued on. The race was an absolute cracker, something we had not seen in a very long time, throughout any tier of racing, but the finish was the bit that shone above all else. As they exited the last corner two wide and chasing down the start finish line, disappearing behind the garages, we had only the voice of the commentator to feed us the result. When he announced that it was so close that they needed to use a photo as they crossed the line just to verify the result, we were shocked! Neither of us had ever heard that before. As it turned out Jonathan Lisseter beat Eddie Mawer by 0.003 seconds. Both Ross and I were stunned, left speechless for a good minute or so, eventually collecting ourselves up and deciding to head back to the car for some lunch.

Following the highly eventful race 1, we thought we'd be onto a winner trying to find people to talk to, as in the formulae we are used to, following a race, all the crew members herd to their car to undertake preparations before sending the car out for the next session; however, in these pocket rockets, that simply wasn't the case! We took another wander through the paddock and once again, everyone had retired to their motorhomes after simply fueling their cars and checking tyre pressures – we couldn't believe how lax everything was, not having to rush around for an hour checking every last bolt and level in the car, seemed wrong somehow! But unfortunately, we were once again unlucky enough to find no drivers to pick the brains of, so we headed for the grandstands at Murrays to watch the second race.

Race 2. Both of us were in firm agreement that race 1 was a bit of a fluke, and this was going to be much more sensible and civilized, and certainly wasn't going

to come down to a sub-1-second finish.... We may have been wrong once again! From our new vantage point, we could see the cars leaving the holding area and heading to the grid. We were thrown when the cars didn't do a warm up lap, just straight to the grid and away they went! We'd gotten to Agostini slightly late for the first race, so just assumed we'd missed it. The flag dropped and the hard racing resumed just like a continuation of the first. Once again, no contact, no funny business, just good hard competition throughout the field. When it came to the final lap, and we once again saw the protagonists from the first race side-by-side down the start finish straight, to finish 0.05 seconds apart, this time in a reversed order, we could not believe our eyes! We'd just watched two races where the winner was sat side-by-side with the bloke in second as they crossed the line. It's firm to say that our minds on whether this formula was the one for us or not, was made up!

CHAPTER 3 – "DO YOU WANT TO BUILD A RACECAR?"

Date: Early December 2022

Time: Evening-ish

Location: At home, sat in the office

It's early December '22, the late nights have drawn in and I'm sitting in the office at home, just off the phone with one of my new best mates! The jolly we took up to Snetterton seems like a long time ago and preparations are now well underway for the 2023 season, so how about a little catch up.

Following the day in Norfolk, Ross and I reached out to the lovely people at the 750 Motor Club, and the Ma7da Championship. We were put in touch with Ben Powney and David Winter, the driver representative and technical representative for the formula. At this point in time, Ross and I were still very much unsure what our intentions were going to be for sourcing our cars, but we assumed speaking to the people in the know would be the best starting point. Ben and Dave (as well as everyone else we spoke with) could not have been more helpful and quickly found us a small handful of options for a variety of budgets. Unfortunately, given mine and Ross' histories, our requirements for cars were a little more specific than most, which led to most of these cars not quite fitting the bill. I think we spoke with about 5 or 6 different people about different cars, but none of them hit the spot.

After all of our searching, we made the call that building our own cars was the option we wished to pursue as that should save us quite a chunk of cash, as well as allowing us to build the cars exactly how we wanted them. We had all but agreed a pair of chassis to pick up, which we had even made a plan for collecting – a round-trip across most of England and Wales, collecting the two chassis, engines for both, gearboxes, axles, panels and various other spares. I believe this was the Thursday before we were due to collect on the Saturday where I reached out to Ben and David once again enquiring about roll cages. It was at this point that he put us in touch with a young gentleman named Alan Coller. Alan, if you don't know, is a legend in the Locost world, having spent a number of years making and developing chassis for the Ford and Mazda Locosts, with a custom roll cage of his own design to go with it.

Cut back to that early December night, 2022 – I have just got off the phone with Alan and agreed the manufacture of 2 brand new chassis for Ross and I, complete with everything to go with it – wishbones, engine mounts and so on. This option – which we were massively glad to hear about just before we spent lots of money on what very well could have been the wrong bits – allowed us to build the cars exactly as we wanted, but also guaranteeing that the chassis we started with are completely straight. Unfortunately, however, a man of Alan's skillset comes in demand, and because of this, he was fully booked until mid-January to start on our chassis, needing 3 weeks for each. No matter, we thought, get the orders in, start sourcing parts, building engines and such, and then go mad throwing it all together once the chassis turns up and try to get the cars built for the first meeting at Croft – what could go wrong!

The following weeks flew by, sourcing a pair of engines each (and might I just add, only spending £650 for the pair of mine – win!), gearboxes, rear axles, diffs, wheels, tyres, brakes – you name it. Unfortunately, due to personal commitments, Ross very quickly had to accept that him making the start of the season was going to be a struggle, so it was agreed that the first chassis ready would be mine so I can still try and make it out to Croft.

January 6th, 2023

People often say that they can remember certain events as clearly as day, and they will probably be able to remember those dates until the day they die – no doubt that you, the reader, have a number yourself. I also have those memories, some fond – the day I proposed to my girlfriend, Bex – some, less fond shall we say (the weekend we spent at Pembrey in the pouring rain with no awning, changing a grand total of 3 gearboxes on 1 car within qualifying and 2 races certainly springs to mind!). This memory however, was one of the exciting ones for sure. I can take you to the exact spot, and explain exactly what I was doing as my phone buzzed with a new email. It was a fairly standard Thursday afternoon, but Bex and I were off skiing that weekend, and I had waited nearly 6 weeks for my new chassis, which was due to be started the following week. The email in question was from Alan Coller, and his email explained that one of the chassis he'd built late in 2022 had come up for sale, no work undertaken on it, just primed, and put in storage. He said he hadn't bought the materials for both chassis yet, and would more than happily cancel the second build if we wanted to buy this one. I jumped with excitement, only to come crashing down to earth! We were heading off at roughly midday on Saturday and the chassis was on the other side of the country – bollocks!

Fortunately, though, my partner in crime also jumped at the opportunity and quickly agreed to buy the chassis.

Home from the week of sunning ourselves in the -20°C temperatures of Finland and I was chomping at the bit, inviting myself over to Ross' to have a first look at the new toy! It may have looked a little drab in the dark-olive-green primer coat that the previous owner had given it, but to the two of us, it looked like opportunity. Plus, it gave us the perfect excuse to get in (Ross on the driver's side of course, it was his car after all) and make the broom-broom noises! Safe to say, I got home that night with a rather big smile on my face – excitement was certainly brewing for the new season of racing.

The following couple of weeks were filled with the last of the big-buys. The engine and diff had been stripped, cleaned, and rebuilt; the ECU had been ordered; I had been put in touch with another couple of new friends-to-be, Stuart Sellars and Dave Boucher. Stuart runs a team called Team Sellars Racing, and they make a lot of bits for the Locosts and Ma7das – if you need a car, speak with Stuart, he has it all! Dave Boucher was suggested by a couple of people, and especially Alan, as the two had worked together on a number of builds before and got on well. Dave sources a number of the parts for the cars, and was more than happy to help a fellow West-countryman (although, between you and me, and given his location, I was reluctant to call him a west-countryman; I had to go past Bristol to get to his workshop, and if you ask me, going past Bristol means you've gone "Up North"!). Joking aside though, Dave was (and still is might I add) an absolute hero! He sourced a load of the last big bits for me, and later in the build was absolutely crucial in getting us out, but I'll get to that later. Either way, he is a top bloke in my books.

Stuart was able to make us up a couple of looms for myself and Ross, as he has been known as the go-to guy for these cars. Dave sourced the shocks, radiator, tonneau cover, rear brakes, exhaust, and a handful of other bits. I was able to head up to meet him one night after work and get a look at some of the cars he had in the workshop before we picked mine up about a week or so later. The cars looked absolutely stunning, and I couldn't wait to get ours to a similar state.

Back at the start of this book, I mentioned my early morning start on the 4th of February – the day that was originally pencilled in for collecting the chassis. I cannot stress how pencilled this day was – nothing was ever confirmed, and there were a lot of things in the air. The chassis was ready, but there were a couple of bits that Alan was waiting to get back from the platers. It wasn't confirmed until early on the 3rd that collecting the following day was off the cards, as I didn't want to rush Alan unnecessarily and we could wait another week. Dad was also unavailable to join me on that date, so it would have been me on my own doing the round trip, so all the cards just added up to put it off by a week. But in doing this, we got what I had been eagerly waiting for. It felt like it was years since I'd agreed the chassis with Alan, but we finally had a date in stone to collect my brand-new race car, and it was only a week away!

CHAPTER 4 – THE END OF AN ERA

Date: 27/12/2022

Time: 11:00

Location: The Garage

Dad and I made the journey to Norfolk on October 29th, 2017, to collect what then was a bare Mallock Mk27 chassis – my next "winter project". A mere 1,885 days later, it left my workshop under its new ownership. During it's time with me, it went through a total of 3 different engines, the same in gearboxes and not a particularly impressive amount of race finishes. As a very young and naïve engineer, I was hoping to use this car as a bit of an "engineering project" to teach myself a number of skills, with the added bonus of getting to race it at the end. Well for sure, that car definitely taught me a lot – countless skills that you just can't gain without getting your hands dirty! Unfortunately, however, one lesson that it not only taught me, but drilled into my brain on a near-daily basis, was that fragile, single-seater cars require a hell of a lot more time, effort, and money than one young man can reasonably provide on his own. Despite the countless hours and friends and family, these things take a lot of work. Work I was certainly more than happy to put in, but work nonetheless. This led to the inevitable yearn for a simpler (and cheaper!) racing life, so after all the time, effort, blood, sweat, tears, cups of tea, late night dominos orders and biscuits, the decision was made to let the ol' girl go.

The young gentleman and his team arrived bright and early on the 27th of December, 2022, after their long journey down from the midlands to collect their car. Armed with a small fleet of vehicles, they loaded it up, as well as the years of spares I had accrued, and took off. His plans were to get the car ready to compete in 2023, again in the Clubmans Sports Prototype Championship, this time however, with a slightly more sensible engine for the size of the car. I wished him the best of luck, and hoped we would meet again sometime soon, so I could get a look at what they achieve. Fortunately, it didn't take too long.

July 15th, 2023

Despite no longer being involved in the championship, I made a number of friends in the Clubmans, so liked to keep updated with how things are going. Flicking through the latest update from their Facebook page, I noticed a car that looked jolly familiar, donning a new all-red livery! Some closer inspection (and a couple of more detailed photographs sent to me later that day) showed what-was my Mallock in a beautiful red livery, driven by its new owner! What a sight it was, hopefully we get the chance to see it in the flesh sometime soon! But for now, all the best to Peter and his new car, I'm looking forward to keeping up with his progress.

CHAPTER 5 – NEW BEGINNINGS

Date: 11/02/2023

Time: 04:00

Location: Home

They say that excitement levels can rarely be beaten as those of a child on Christmas morning, well whoever it was that said that is wrong – very wrong! It was another early start for us, but as you're probably getting the gist of by now, when it comes to racing cars and living in the South West, that's just something you learn to live with. After a couple of months of preparations and waiting, we were finally heading across to the South East to collect the freshly build chassis from Alan. Neatly laid out in the workshop was the freshly rebuild engine, gearbox, diff, and the mountain of shiny new bits that had been getting delivered almost daily for the build (side note, massive shout-out to my neighbours for not getting annoyed with the amount of big, heavy things that kept getting left with them while no-one was home! I bought them a bottle of wine to say both sorry and thank you – hopefully they don't hate me too much).

The main reason Dad and I left as early as we did, was because one of the things Alan was doing was modifying mine and Ross' rear axles with the required suspension mounts, so we needed to give him plenty of time to do those mods.

We arrived with Alan at about 9am, made initial introductions with him and his family, and began loading the parts into the van and onto the trailer while he started on the rear axles. Given the time Alan needed on each of the axles, Dad and I had plenty of time to admire the true craftsmanship in the chassis – everything about it beautifully formed and immaculately welded together. More a work of art than a racing car, would be such a shame to put this in the fence, turn 1 at Croft! Up until this point, Dad hadn't been massively involved with the preparations for the car. He knew the plan, and helped me with the engine and diff, but otherwise, was still quite in the dark about it all mechanically. I'd made a bit of a plan leading up to today, and agreed with everyone that myself and Dad were going to be very unavailable for the months to come – I think secretly, Dad was excited to get stuck into this new project, but as usual, reading him was much akin to punching water (I.E. that it's pointless, or that you look stupid doing it!).

We spent a good couple of hours going through each and every nook and cranny of the car and the impending build; what we needed to do, when we needed it done by, what help I needed from him, etc. Come midday, Alan was all but nearly finished with the axles, and we had made a firm game plan for getting the car together.

Come about 2pm, everything was finished, we thanked Alan and his family for their time and hospitality, and hit the road, homeward-bound. I don't recall how long the journey home was, but I can remember clear as day, that there wasn't a quiet moment all afternoon long. Constant questions back and forth, covering any and all basis of the car, and our hopes of (somehow) trying to get the car ready for the first meeting. All in all, though, confidence was high – an unimaginable amount of effort went into the car before I had even laid eyes on it, we'd planned every eventuality, had most of the parts ready to go straight onto the car and the paint was ready to go onto the chassis. As we locked the garage that night, we were prepared for what was to come.

CHAPTER 6 – DAY 1, 61 DAYS UNTIL CROFT

Date: 12/02/2023

Time: Early!

Location: The Garage (where else!)

I can't remember when the garage was unlocked that morning, but I know for sure, it was damp, dark, and cold. Day 1 was an important day in the build – Dad and I both work full time and weren't blessed with the luxury of taking weeks off to get the racecar ready, which meant that if we were going to get this thing done in time, every spare minute of every day was absolutely critical. Collecting the chassis on a Saturday wasn't just a lucky fluke, it was planned so we had Sunday to do what needed doing, before painting the chassis, and all other parts, the following nights after work.

We'd agreed our roles the day before – Dad and I can both weld fairly well, but only one of us knew where all the brackets I'd designed and had made for mounting the panels would fit on the chassis. Therefore, most of the day was spent with me hastily putting things into place with magnets, while Dad followed me and welded them into place. In his off-time, he went around the car and gave it a light key with some wet and dry in preparation for primer the following night. Come the end of the evening, when the light of day had come and gone, the chassis was fully prepped and rubbed down ready for the first coat of paint the following night.

During the winter, it is normally really hard to muster the enthusiasm to get into the garage. When you've been at work all day, you're tired, and it's basically dark as you leave (and was also dark when you got there that morning), putting in another few hours can be tough. Funnily enough, we didn't struggle on this evening, or many that followed! Monday night, Tuesday night, Wednesday night, they came, they went! Primer, red paint, black paint, white paint, blue paint; we coated every corner of the workshop in overspray, but come Friday night, we had a full car's worth of brackets, a large number of panels and various other odds and sods ready to get chucked on the car.

The car had not been in its new home for a week, and it was already looking glorious in a striking shade of red. The first full weekend of building was now upon us, and this could be our first challenge – fitting the engine and gearbox. With these Locost chassis, they have a "spine" through the centre of them, which means you need to have the gearbox bolted onto the engine and fit the two together. Alan had supplied the engine mounts, and said what gearbox mounts the car was designed for, which I had purchased ahead of time. Offer the assembly into the car, get the engine mounts in – success! "Right, let's get the gearbox mount in" ……." oh s***!!!". For reasons unbeknownst to us, the gearbox mount wasn't fitting. We made calls to all of our new contacts hoping someone would be able to point us in the right direction, but unfortunately, everyone said that everything looked about right, and no one was in a position to check dimensions of things on their own cars. We always knew there was going to be trouble somewhere along the way, we'd just hoped it might have been a little further down the road! No matter, there was still a long list of things that could get fitted to the car, so we got our heads down and cracked on with the list.

The weekend flew by, and before we knew, Monday was upon us, which meant I could contact the supplier of my gearbox mount to get some confirmation of dimensions. Fortunately, they were able to see the issue almost straight away and commented that they had sent an old-revision part out by accident. They would happily send a replacement straight away, but it would be another day or so wait. A day or so wait, we haven't got time like that to play around with! Fortunately, they were able to confirm the correct dimension so I could introduce said bracket to a good friend of mine – the angle grinder! After a brief, but concise discussion, the bracket decided to play ball and fit absolutely perfectly! This meant that after another (and certainly not the last) late night, the engine and box were now fully mounted in the car, very exciting!

As the days turned quickly into weeks, the pile of parts on the floor of the workshop was diminishing at an astronomical rate and it wasn't much longer before we started introducing panels to the car, and the new machine was starting to take shape. Fortunate as this was, the clock was still ticking away ever faster – 31 days until Croft.

CHAPTER 7 – "IT'S LOOKING A BIT TOUCH-AND-GO NOW."

Date: 01/04/2023

Time: 02:30 (yep, AM)

Location: Home

> "No matter how airtight you make a plan, somewhere along the way, something will

> come along and puncture it somehow"
> – Me, trying to cleverly (I think that's
> a word) sum up the situation.

It was a brilliant plan. Buy chassis and all parts to fit onto it. Source panels, mod panels, mould panels, make new panels, fit panels. Unfortunately, life would be boring if it were that simple.

It was about a month to go, leading up to the first meeting at Croft. Dad and I had put in a monumental effort to get the car to where it was, but it looked as though all of that effort could well be in vain. Ross was very luckily able to get his hands on a full set of panels for a Locost for an absolute steal. Bought the panels, tested them on the car, they fit a treat, moulded them, and made new ones for me. We always knew the bonnet was going to be a tricky little bugger, because on these cars, with the larger Mazda engine, you need to cut the bonnet and fit a bulge around the top of the engine. Our plan was to use the bonnet Ross had got in his kit, mod as required, and go from there. Unfortunately, it turned out that the bonnet was slightly different to the "standard" Ma7da panels that everyone was using, and with the appropriate amount cut out, was about half as tall as it should be – big problem! We made countless calls once again to our new friends for anyone to help with getting a solution, and it wasn't until I spoke with Stuart Sellars again that we were able to find one. Stuart was our savior here, and was able to make me a new bonnet, bulge, and nosecone to the "Ma7da" spec which should (pretty much) fit straight onto our car! He needed a couple of weeks to do it, but once we got the panels, they should fit straight on. Amazing! The perfect solution, we are getting a little close for comfort once the 2-weeks has passed, but the panels will drop straight on and away we go!

Again, the two weeks vanished in the blink of an eye, and we were discussing options for getting the panels delivered down from Boston to Exeter. Annoyingly however, given the size of the package, Stuart couldn't get them down to us until the following Thursday, which was a day after we were booked in for shaking the car down at Llandow, and only a week before we needed to be ready for Croft. I therefore asked, "could I run up and collect them" to which he said "Of course".

So, it's 2:30am, I'm sat on my driveway in the car, ready to drive 6 hours up the road, pick up some panels, drive 6 hours back, then go about butchering them for the rest of the day and making them fit. I pulled up outside TSR's workshop at about half 8, said "Hi" to Stuart and Daniel Cort (one of the drivers in the Ma7da championship, who I would later be racing with), threw the panels in the boot of Clifford, before nailing it back home and getting to the workshop for about 2:30pm ish. Dad had been there all day at this point, and couldn't quite understand how I'd done 12 hours of driving and 530 miles, and still be home for early afternoon, ready for a full-on afternoon of chopping up a brand-new set of panels! Amazing what you can achieve when you put your mind to something.... plus, enough Monster to wake the dead!

Amazingly, given that this was the biggest issue we had faced thus-far in the build, we had managed to get around the problem, and although it wasn't pretty, we had a full set of panels on the car ready for our shakedown later that week. Nothing was painted, but that didn't matter! We had much bigger issues on our hands!

CHAPTER 8 – "IT'S GOT FUEL, IT'S GOT COMPRESSION…"

Date: 05/04/2023

Time: Well past midnight

Location: I'll give you one guess!

It was an almighty effort! An unholy effort! We had never tasked ourselves with something like this before, and were amazed we had made it as far as we did, but those racing gods are little buggers sometimes.

While I was having a jolly around central England picking up panels, Dad was working on a slightly more pressing issue. We had everything wired up, plumbed together, but the engine wasn't firing. We had tried everything we could think of, but there was no spark. You need 3 things for an internal combustion engine to work; fuel, compression, and spark, and although Meatloaf may think that 2 out of 3 ain't bad, unfortunately that doesn't fly in the automotive world.

Fortunately for us, after nights wasted trying different things, we thought to try Ross' wiring loom, which we had in the workshop. Amazingly, with only 3 spark plugs in the engine, the other being used to test for spark, the engine did its best to try and start - at last! We threw the final plug back in the engine and tried again and the sheer bliss in the air when the Mazda lump roared into life, we had finally done it! Panels were done, now the engine ran, amazing! It was now Tuesday night, the Tuesday night before the shakedown on Thursday and we only now actually thought we might be able to really make it to Croft next weekend. Eager to prove it worked, I jumped in the driver's seat and took the car for its first spin around the yard. The rain had started coming down, but we didn't care, the months of hard work had finally paid off....or so we thought.

After a couple of laps of gently pootling the car up and down the yard, it didn't take long for it to start misfiring and struggling to run. We checked everything over, but couldn't work out what was going wrong.

By now, it was late Tuesday night, Dad and I were both working the following day, and we really should have called it a night, but we had to keep trying, we needed to find the problem that was stopping the engine from running! Once again, I started making phone calls. Anyone who might be able to offer that little nugget of information as to why the car wasn't running. Every time someone suggested something as the cause, I told Dad, and he would start working on that part while I finished on the phone. Almost every time it was suggested that we had a leaky manifold, but no leak was found. Eventually it was well past midnight, and we had to call it a day. Maybe we would have better luck Wednesday night, but my god did we need to find it Wednesday night!

Unfortunately, no one could think of what could be causing the engine to run so badly, we had people on standby to take the car to who could plug the ECU in to check all the sensors were working correctly, we went through absolutely every part of the fuel and electrical system and couldn't see any problems – we were completely stuck! And on the night before we were due to go testing. No words could describe how we felt as we locked up the garage. The closest we got was that the engine ran ok until it got to about 60°C. Maybe if I bought a new temperature sensor tomorrow morning when the shops open, and that fixes it, that we can make it to Llandow (about 3 hours away from us) for a couple of hours running in the afternoon? Maybe, just maybe!

At about half past 11, Dad and I locked up the workshop and called it a day. On the brief journey home, I had a message from Dave Boucher asking how we had got on. I went back to him explaining that we had had no luck, and I was going to try this that and whatever tomorrow morning, but had to wait until the shops opened first, and he wished me the best of luck and apologized that he couldn't help more.

April 6th, 2023 – Shakedown day

I was up at the crack of dawn. I had little-to-no sleep all night. I couldn't sleep, who in their right mind would be able to sleep right about now! We should be on the road at this exact moment heading to Llandow to go testing and we couldn't get the car working. I had been through every single part of the fuel and electrical system again and again in my head to try and work out what could be causing the problem, if not the temperature sensor as we suspected.

The phone rings – Dave Boucher.

It was about 6am, he should be asleep, not ringing me!

A: "Good morning, Dave. How are you doing?"

D: "I'm good ta, you?"

A: "As you can probably imagine, I've been better!"

D: "Well how about I suggest something that will cheer you up then?"

A: "Go for it"

D: "How have you plumbed up your fuel pressure regulator?"

As he said that, a light switched on in my head! He was dead right, how had I plumbed up my fuel pressure regulator! As it turned out, on these pressure regulators, there is a side with a push-fit fitting, and one with a screw-fit fitting. I had (stupidly) assumed (as there were no instructions) that the screw fit fitting was the outlet (going to the high-pressure line), and the push fit, the inlet (coming from the pump), which is completely wrong. I will admit, I had never felt more of a moron in my life than I did in that moment! I hastily thanked Dave for his wisdom and raced down the garage. Swapped the fuel lines as fast as I could and fired the car up. Waiting anxiously for the car to reach 60°C where it normally started hunting, but this time, nothing – a perfect clean idle all the way to 85°C. Halle-goddamn-lugah!

Not 5 minutes later, I was on the phone with Dad; "pack your bags and bring the van, we are going testing!"

CHAPTER 9 – THE SECRET SIGNAL

Date: 06/04/2023

Time: 11:45

Location: Llandow Circuit

We managed to get to Llandow with 15 minutes remaining of the morning session. We thought "balls to it! We've come this far, let's see if we can get a quick blast in before the lunch break". Speaking with the track official and explaining our situation, he gladly came over, noise tested the car and had a quick look over it while I was putting my "jamas" on. He gave us the go-ahead and let us out on track. Unfortunately, however, someone – who shall remain nameless – was a little pre-occupied with the whole situation of the last 12 hours, checking everything on the car, and generally rushing a little more than he should. There was one car on track – a classic mini race car, which I noted pass the pit lane, and proceeded to pull out onto the track, knowing it was safe, but not noticing the red light at the end of the paddock. 1 lap in, and shown the black flag – bollocks!

I pulled into the pits and apologised to the marshal – he understood and told me not to do it again, and we got on with the matter at hand. By the time we had faffed around with that, there was only time for about 5 minutes of running, but the beauty of a short circuit like Llandow, is 5 minutes of running feels like the equivalent to about 50 laps. We never timed a lap around Llandow (as it never seemed relevant), but it can't be too far off a 50 second lap at a guess. So, we nailed in as many laps as we could before the chequered flag flew, indicating the end of the morning running. As I pulled into the paddock, the car seemingly working fairly flawlessly, I could feel the pain in my cheeks as my grin touched both ears! Finally, 54 days of flat out pushing, and we managed to get out for testing. I couldn't believe it.

Mum and Dad both accompanied me to Llandow for the afternoon. Unfortunately, Bex had to work, so she was waiting eagerly at the other end of the phone to hear how we were getting on throughout the day. Llandow is a very small track nestled away in the Welsh countryside. The people there are lovely, and they hold open testing most weekdays for people with a racing licence. At a very minimal cost compared to normal trackdays, this is the perfect place to go and take a car for shaking down when you get them first built. We took the Mallock here a couple of times, but as was usually the way with it, struggled with reliability. We were hoping today wasn't going to follow the same fate.

After returning to the pits following the brief running at the end of the morning session, Dad jumped to the car. As we had for most of the build, we'd made a plan for our intentions of the day much before getting to the track that morning. I'd bought 10 tyres for the car – you aren't limited to how many tyres you can use in a year, and at only £80 ish each, they were very reasonably priced compared to normal racing tyres. Our thoughts were to have a set of scrubbed tyres ready to go that we can bolt on should the heavens open before a race (as we use the same tyres for wet and dry conditions). Dad swapped all the tyres around and bolted on the set which (although I didn't know at the time) would last us until the halfway point of the season. As well as the tyres, we had a really good check over the whole car. Given how long it had taken us to put the thing together, we were adamant there was going to be at least one thing on the car that would come loose on the bumpy terrain here in Wales. However, checking everything over and there was nothing found to be wrong! We even double checked just to be sure, as we couldn't believe it. Therefore, we assumed everything to be good, made a cup of tea and took a little breather before the afternoon running began.

The lunch hour passed, and the afternoon running began. The sun was shining, but it was rather windy at the track, so ideal testing weather for a car I'd barely driven before. We were fairly certain it was going to be soaking rain all day, but we got very lucky, with just a very light sprinkling towards the end of the day. There were 4 other cars with us that day – the classic mini I mentioned before, a pair of race-prepped Honda Civic Mk7's, and a mad looking Lotus race car thing (which unfortunately didn't get much running in the afternoon as they broke something in the morning and struggle to get it fixed at the track). Us not getting there until late in the afternoon seemed to be a blessing in disguise as most of the other teams didn't do much running in the afternoon, and were all gone by about 2:30-3:00pm ish, which gave us a good few hours of running where we were the only people there.

As I slipped my helmet back on once more, Dad and I discussed our plan for the afternoon running,

ONE TYRE FIRE

and we both agreed that seat time was the most important thing by a country mile; therefore, the plan was for me to go out and just put laps in, play with the brake bias and just generally get a feel for the car, and they would call me in after I'd done 15 minutes – the length of a race in our formula. I jumped into the car, fired it up and pulled out onto the track for the first run of the afternoon.

Llandow is a very short, bumpy track – it's not overly technical, but the short sharp nature of it really tests a car quite nicely, and it allows you to get a really good feel for it with its variety of corners. The lap starts with a long (I say long, it's not long, but it's long given the length of the track) run down the start/finish straight, with the pits and paddock area on your left. Gently drift the car over to the right as you head down the straight ready for the first corner, a bus stop complex of a left, right, right, left, right – all pretty much taken as one corner! Gauge your braking on the markers and the control tower sat on the apex of the first corner and stand on the brakes as hard as you can! Down from 4th to 3rd and 2nd, turn in, hit the apex, then throw the car right to hit apexes 2 and 3, feed in the throttle (gently) and dart right to get a good line for the next left. By now you are hard on the throttle, dart left to get a good run through the final right, hit the apex, change into 3rd, run the kink left before feathering the car through the next corner, the right hander onto the back straight. It may only be testing, but what kind of racing driver wouldn't be testing the limits on a racing track! Slide the car through the fast right onto the back straight, select 4th and keep the car pinned to the left down the straight. Quick check of the gauges before preparing for the final complex. Gauge the braking, hit the pedal hard, down to 3rd, chuck the car in, right, left, right and run the car out wide coming into the final corner. Hard on the throttle on the short straight into the last corner, before lifting off and feathering again through the long last right hander to take you once again onto the start / finish straight. Be careful not to get too excited on the long and appealing run off area to carry more speed – there ain't much grip out there, ask me how I know! Onto the main straight now, hard on the loud pedal and into 4th before you do it all over again! It may not be the most complicated track, but do that 20-odd times in a race distance and it really takes it out of you. I would love to come back here for a race meeting at some point in the future - 20 odd cars rattling around here would be absolutely incredible! That may be a pipedream though.

When the 15 minute "race" had finished, Mum or Dad would take turns standing by the wall in the paddock and doing the Team America "Secret Signal" to me to come into the pits. I was told to judge them on the way home, and deemed that

Dad's was better, as it made me laugh right as I was heading into turn 1, which led to a massive lock up, and completely bailing on even attempting to make the first corner!

The car was absolutely singing in the first session. There were a couple of small setup changes that I wanted to make, but nothing drastic, I was just loving getting the feel for the new car. Therefore, we opted not to change anything, re-fuelled and went straight back out again. The second run I had a bit more of an eye in for the car, what it could and couldn't do, and therefore tried to treat it more like an actual race. Did a quick "warm up" lap before then pushing hard for the rest of the session. Brake balance was something I was playing around with all afternoon, never quite getting it "just right". There was a small period during this session where I had locked up and missed the first complex for about 4 laps straight – so much so I noticed the track marshal look out and watch me for the next couple of laps. At this point, I was the only car on track, so wasn't putting anyone at risk, and was being very cautious as I rejoined the track anyway, but I thought it an act of self-preservation to be a little more delicate in the laps to follow. Eventually, towards the end of this session, I managed to get the brakes somewhere a little bit better, and could settle down for some more fast laps.

15 minutes once again came and went, and the

secret signal was deployed. Again, not wanting to waste time, we refuelled the car and gave it a check over while I had a quick drink myself, and we hopped back to work.

The third session however was a little shorter than usual. I headed out onto the track, made it only as far as the back straight when the bonnet tried its best to come off! I slowed right down and crawled back to the pits where Mum and Dad were a little puzzled with why I'd backed off. I said about the bonnet, and mere moments later, Dad had dug out some blue rope and strapped the bonnet back into place – good enough to last the rest of the day at least! Right, let's try that again!

Much like the sessions before, and after the bonnet mishap, the 3rd and 4th sessions went off without a hitch! I was getting more and more confident in the car with every lap, and loving how it was driving. We had no mechanical trouble all day long, and the only issue coming from a, umm, "fuel pressure issue" shall we say! After getting towed back to the pits, we filled the tank again and it ran fine.

The days running was due to end at 5pm, and by the time we had finished our 4th session, it was half 4. At this point, we had done an estimated 100 laps of the track, and firing on only a couple of hours sleep, I was knackered. That being said however, I still wanted more. We didn't have enough fuel left for a complete run, so we made a best judgement call on how much running we could get – estimating about 10 minutes – emptied the rest of our fuel into the tank and went for one last run. This would be the last time I drove the car before Croft the following weekend, so I wanted to make sure I had gotten absolutely everything I could out of the afternoon at Llandow. Therefore, I tried one last time to push the boat out on how fast I could get this little beast around the track. I pushed harder than I had all day, and it felt like I'd gone faster, but as mentioned, we weren't timing, so I'll never know! I was inevitably called back to the pits after the 10 minutes was up, and we put the car back on the trailer and packed up.

Given that 12 hours before the car went back onto the trailer at the track, it wasn't running properly and we were fairly certain we were missing the days testing, to manage to get out at all was a miracle, and to get out and see no mechanical issues all day was just beyond belief! We couldn't believe it, and the van was absolutely buzzing the whole way home. Unfortunately, however, despite how amazing the day had turned out to be, that didn't mean it was over. We now had 1 week before the car had to be ready to go for Croft, and the bonnet was still a mess, we needed to paint half the panels, it needed stickers, we needed to sort some new bonnet pins, setup – the list was huge. No matter though, after what we had achieved that day, we were adamant that nothing was going to stop us now.

CHAPTER 10 – CAN I ASK A FAVOUR?

Date: 10/04/2023

Time: 17:00

Location: The Garage

The success of our day at Llandow was still pulsing through my veins. I still couldn't believe it – the stupid plan we had come up with the best part of half a year ago was finally coming together and I'd got my first laps in the car - I was buzzing. That did not mean that we could back off the throttle and relax for the week however – we still had a lot of things that needed doing. And just as luck would have it, this weekend I was away at a friend's Stag Do, just what I needed the week before the first meeting with extreme time pressure against us.

The plan for the week was simple enough, but by no means easy. By the time I was home from the Stag Do, I was unable to get any time down the garage, meaning the Monday night was the first time I could get down there since the test day on Thursday, therefore:

Monday: Sort the panels and prime them, fix the slight leak on the hydraulic handbrake, sort the gearstick, bolt check and level check.

Tuesday: Paint the panels (unfortunately my workshop isn't flush with space, so a job like painting the panels requires the whole garage, and leaving them to dry means we can't crack on with anything else)

Wednesday: Call up a mahoosive favour to our friend Ian the signwriter and get him to quickly whip us up some stickers for the car. Also, fill the van with fuel, go food shopping, get race fuel for the car, sort overnight bag and throw together as many spares and tools as we think we will need for the weekend. Plus, anything else we had forgotten!

Thursday: GO TO CROFT!

So yeah, not the easiest of job lists given the time frame. We called in favours with everyone we knew who could help in any way possible – I think I spent more money on thank you beers that week than I had the last month on the car. But, as if by some kind of miracle, we managed everything and Thursday night, we were in the van heading for Croft. Dad and I struggled to believe that we had actually done it until about the time we pulled in the gates at the track. It had taken us the grand total of 61 days to go from a bare, brand-new chassis, to a completed, painted, ready to race, car. It was by no means perfect, with a host of things that wanted changing, fixing, or updating for the next meeting, but we didn't care, we had done it!

CHAPTER 11 – "I'M PRETTY SURE I NEARLY DROWNED OUT THERE!"

Date: 14/04/2023

Time: 02:00

Location: Croft Circuit

ONE TYRE FIRE

The journey to Croft hadn't been the easiest. It was simple running for most of the journey, but about 2 hours from the track, Dad asked if I would take over driving the van as he was getting tired. This is normally how we work when heading to race meetings, one of us handles the first slog as we leave straight from work, and then swap when appropriate. This time however, I feel I had been dealt the short straw! We swapped drivers and Dad sat in the back and had a little nap. I was knackered – we'd spent 2 months doing late nights and early starts, worked full time (only taking one day off for the testing at Llandow might I add), and worked all day that Thursday before we left for Croft. I was more than ready for this weekend to be over just so I could start to catch up on some sleep.

Just as luck would have it however, this weekend was when Highways England decided to create a massive diversion off the main road to the track, and through towns and villages, on some "less than ideal" roads. With Dad asleep in the back, and it being midnight in a part of the country I've never been before, this diversion was really not what I needed. Fortunately, I had the trusty sat-nav going – surely that will help me get through this. Well, the diversion signs simply ceased in the middle of a little village right before a roundabout, and the sat nav was telling me to turn around and go back the way I came. I ended up taking a gamble and hoping it would work out, and as luck would have it, it did and eventually the sat nav caught up and got us back on track. After all that, and the last hour of peace, we pulled up at Croft at about 2:00am and parked up in the paddock. There was testing on the Friday, hence why we left of the Thursday night, but even so, the paddock was full, and having only met a handful of people at different points, we didn't know where we could land. Therefore, I just dumped it at one end, we'd sort it in the morning. We went to the loo and crashed, excited for the 3 or 4 hours of sleep we were getting.

Morning broke out and we were greeted by the sun shining, a bit of wind, and not a cloud in the sky! As luck would have it, the motorhome we had parked up next to belonged to Lucas Batt and his team, who were being run by none other than my new mate, Dave Boucher. He therefore helped us move the barriers around so we could setup and make camp for the weekend. We got the car off the trailer, and it wasn't long before a fleet of people, drivers and crew were wandering over, introducing themselves and have a nosey at the car. We'd only been here for a couple of hours, and already people were making us feel at home – lovely! It wasn't long before the Tannoy came to life and the different groups were getting called to the holding area for their sessions. We were session "C", so we had a good hour or so extra to get the car ready to go, stickered up, and prepped for the first session.

"Group C testing to the holding area please – all cars for Group C testing to holding please, thank you".

Croft is a beautiful circuit, really one of the gems of UK motorsport. It's a very fast and technical track, that really tests a driver. Now I am man enough to admit that I was absolutely useless here this weekend. Battling with learning the car, a couple of mechanical teething troubles, and my confidence driving it, there was a lot of time left out there for sure. But I didn't mind, and still don't mind – it was my first meeting in the car, and you have to start somewhere. I've been involved in motorsport for a long time, and know firsthand that if you try too hard in a car you aren't 100% sure about, it can all go wrong very quickly, and Croft is a circuit that will happily chew you up and spit you out if you drive like a tosser, so I knew that I was always going to be a bit reserved this weekend, no matter how hard I tried, I wasn't going to set the screens alight, and I was fine with that – I had the rest of the year to do that!

There were 4x 20-minute testing sessions on for each class, and I was intending on utilising them all, so the first session was always going to be about getting our eye in. We had no idea what we should be doing with setup, tyre pressures, driving style – you name it. This car was so vastly different to anything Dad, or I had driven before that we really didn't know where to start, so we took a stab and thought we could go from there. We also struggled with the brakes – I had them dialled in, but they just weren't doing anything. Then there was the wandering under the brakes. Wandering under braking is where the car naturally steers itself when you brake hard, caused by bump and droop steer. We hadn't been able to go fast enough at Llandow to experience this, so hadn't thought of it as an issue, but at Croft with its big braking zones, it was very noticeable, and quite dangerous. Come the end of the first session, that was the biggest thing that needed fixing! Fortunately, with Alan's infinite wisdom, he has designed slots in the mounting brackets for the steering rack so you can adjust your bump steer. We took a gamble as we were tight on time during the build and put the rack in the middle of the slots. This was clearly wrong, so we jumped up and down on the front axle to see what the wheels were doing, and opted to try it with the rack at the top, hopefully this would help fix the issues.

We made the changes we wanted between the first and second sessions, and headed out once again. The weather was still pretty good for us, so we aimed to capitalise on that and continue learning the track and the car. This session was much better for sure, with the wandering now dialled out, I could try and push myself that bit harder. With the nature of these testing sessions, you get mixed up with cars of different classes, so it is hard to gauge your speed, and occasionally a faster car will appear in your mirror and dart around you, or you'll catch a slower car and have to navigate around them. It's all common stuff, but bloody hell is it annoying when you are trying to work on yourself. Eventually, the chequers flew again, and the session was finished. We pulled back into the paddock and Dad and I discussed how the car was behaving before deciding on the changes we wanted to make to try and make it more drivable. This time we had the lunch break to add to our adjustment time, so we got the car fully prepped, before stopping for a cup of tea and a pasty.

The third session was business as usual, fortunately not coming across any technical issues with the car, and my confidence in it and around the track growing with every passing corner! I was really starting to get the feel for the car and was loving it. Once again, back to the paddock for our final check over before the last session of the day. Confidence in the team was high, and already we were starting to get the gist of the car; working on it in a race setting, changes we could make and how they affected the handling, the fuel usage – all that stuff.

It was at this point that the heavens opened.

As we were doing the final checks on the car,

just about ready to get bolted back in for the last session of the day, the clouds came and they released an almighty downpour on the track. I'd not driven the car in the wet yet, and didn't know how good or bad the tyres would be in these conditions. No matter, nothing that could be done about it now. We softened the car off and headed out, into the unknown. The holding area was full before all of the sessions thus far that day, but heading over for this last session, I was the only car there bar one single seater, prototype car. The marshal let us out and away we went. As it turned out, there were a handful of other Ma7da drivers who ended up joining us for the session, but gave it a minute or so before they headed out, so it wasn't too empty in the end.

My first time driving the car in the wet was less than enjoyable. I normally enjoy wet conditions, but I just couldn't find any grip in this car, constantly catching massive puddles and aquaplaning across the track, very nearly finding the barrier on a series of occasions. I put in 3 extortionately slow laps before eventually deciding that it wasn't worth smashing the car up in testing. We'd come a very long way and I wasn't prepared to risk all of that on my first outing, IN TESTING! I pulled into the pits and said to Dad that I was calling it, it was lethal out there, and wasn't worth the risk. He accepted my decision and we headed back to the paddock. Inside, I was absolutely furious with myself. Had I made the right call? Was I just being a massive woosy-pants? Should I have just stayed out and got the experience in the wet? I got back to the pits and thought to myself about the options, and even considered heading back out again and seeing if I could learn anything else. I switched off the car and climbed out – I was soaking wet top-to-toe. Dad then wandered over and asked for a more detailed explanation of what it was like out there, and as I started to explain, we watched the rest of the Ma7da's that had followed onto the track late, all pull back into the paddock, making the same decision as I – vindication! Dad uttered "I guess coming in was probably the right call after all, if they are all doing the same". That made me feel loads better about my decision. After I'd got changed and we'd checked the car over before the evening, I recalled heading into Sunny-In sideways, pointing at the wall as a small tsunami washed over the side of the car and completely drenched me – it was definitely the right call to bail before I tried a little too hard and put it in the fence. That would not have been at all the right thing to do before even making it to the first race of the weekend!

Later that evening, the rain stopped and the sun came out, giving a lovely warm mid-April evening for us to walk the track and get a better feel for where I could make some improvements. Over the course of our walk, I think we found best part of about 4 seconds, where I was taking lines that just weren't right for the car, realising that maintaining momentum was by far and away the most important thing out there.

Saturday – Qualifying and Race 1.

Morning broke and we were summoned to the scrutineering bay to get our cars checked over. It seems that the formulas of the weekend get chosen at random for scrutineering, and we were on the list this weekend. We also had a drivers briefing that morning too, so a sufficiently busy start to the day, given that we had to squeeze qualifying in too!

The car breezed through scrutineering and before we knew it, we were in the holding area for quali. In this formula, your fastest time determines your starting position for race 1, and your second fastest time gives you race 2; with race 3 being determined by your positions over the two preceding races. Fortunately, the conditions for quali were dry, and we were able to head out and pick up where we left the following day. I was still feeling good in the car, and I was starting to build enough pace to start steering the setup of the car slightly. Unfortunately, however, it turned out that my pace wasn't quite as good as I was hoping, and I qualified third-from-last in both sessions. Not exactly what I was hoping for, but by no means disappointing. There would be people for me to have a mess around with, and hopefully we can learn loads in the first race.

Sat on the grid for Race 1, I could hear my heartbeat as a single, solid sound, rather than a calm beat. I'd not done a standing start in this car yet, and I'd never done a hard launch in a car that doesn't have big sticky slick tyres and a limited slip diff in the back, so I really wasn't confident. How many revs do you give it, how do you release the clutch, how much throttle do you give once you've launched? I thought "f*** it!" and did what I did in the Mallock, gave it 5-6k RPM and dropped the clutch when the lights went out – turns out this approach is very, very wrong! I lit one tyre up like mad, and absolutely nothing from the other – a "One-Tyre-Fire" if you will. Feathering the throttle and quickly but gently as I could to try and calm the back end down, I was stone, cold last as we headed for turn one. I was able to sneak up the inside of a couple of people as we headed for the chicane, but a very loose Lewis Penstone-Smith had lost it going through the chicane and I had to take avoiding action around the outside of him as we headed for the back straight and into Tower corner. So annoyingly, I had ended up all on my own with no one to try and learn off, but that wasn't the biggest issue I was facing.

Despite running near-faultlessly at Llandow and yesterday testing here at Croft, it was at this point that the engine decided to develop a misfire! Not big enough to warrant me pulling off the track, but very annoying nonetheless as the car was popping and banging down the straights, I could see the cars in front pulling length, after length out of me. So, despite my best efforts, this race was going to be a bit of a write off. No matter, there is always more to learn, so I tried my best to maximise the corners and learn what I could there.

After a handful of laps, Lewis had caught and passed me into Sunny-In, so I did my best to try and hang on with him, but it was at this point that the safety car came out, followed by a red flag and a race restart. Callum Barnes had a moment out of the first corner and put the front end into the wall, meaning the recovery team were needed to help move his car out the way. At this point also, Stephen Manley who I'd managed to retake through turn one had pulled off behind me, meaning I was sat in last place on the grid.

Eventually the cars were fired back into life and setup in their new grid positions. I tried my best being a bit gentler this time, but was still way too excited on the throttle and had a start much the same as earlier that race – what I would give for rolling starts eh! Still fighting my misfire, I tried my best to keep up with the cars ahead, but it was not to be. Nonetheless, we crossed the line in 15th and last position (of those still running) and our first race finish of the season! It may not have been a particularly exciting race for us, but it was a finish, and that was good enough for me at that point! We were happy with the handling of the car, but just desperately needed to sort the misfire.

I went to Ben Powney with my issue and he suggested I spoke with another driver, David Bowen. Introductions were made to David and his family, and they were more than happy to help with our car, coming over and plugging it in to their laptop, doing some witchcraft and wizardry that ultimately resulted in the engine sounding happier, healthier and FASTER than it had ever done before, so we were over the moon that Sunday, we could try and push on and get stuck in! We paid David and Sam sufficiently in cider for helping us with the car, and exchanged pleasantries with them for a short while afterwards, with Dad and David reminiscing of the "good ol' days" on the short ovals with the hot rods. Short circuit people always seem to manage to find other short circuit people!

The evening was very pleasant after that, with the sun setting, and the evening offering a gentle warmth. We ate BBQ'ed fish fingers and bacon for dinner that night and took a moment to really understand what we had achieved the last couple of months! It was really something, and we still couldn't believe that not only had we made it, but finished the first race. We were certain that something would go wrong and ruin the day for us one way or another. But alas, that wasn't the case!

It was probably about 8pm ish in the evening, and we were just finishing up our dinner. We were both tired, but I wanted one last walk around the track to try and learn anything else I could before the day tomorrow. We agreed that we would finish up, tidy up and then head for that walk. It's always beneficial to walk the track the night before a meeting I find. When you are flying through a track at race pace, you can't see and feel everything that the track has to offer. Walking it however, you can look for hidden bumps, patches of grip, is the rubber on this kerb, is the grass sticky, marbles – all these little things you just don't see in the car, but when you know about them in the back of your mind, it lets you drive slightly differently knowing that there is or isn't grip in certain places. We've always found it helps, so now whenever we can, we always try and get a walk in to see what we can learn.

Dad got up from his seat in the van to go and grab another bite from the BBQ, and it was at this point that my fiancée, Bex, jumped into the van. Dad and I had come to Croft alone, it was a 6-hour journey, and Bex had football on Saturday, so she had decided not to come to this meeting. So, what in god's name was she doing here? I was amazed and genuinely speechless! She's planned it all along that she was going to watch the football, hit the road and come and meet us up here for the day of racing on Sunday, she'd booked a hotel down the road in secret and made all the arrangements, I had absolutely no words! Still to this day, it puts a smile on my face remembering that moment.

Sunday – Races 2 and 3

As I mentioned previously, we had qualified in the same place for race 2 as race 1. I still hadn't worked out how to get my head around these race starts, so thought I'd try and go a little lower on the revs again. As I sat in the holding area, engine idling lovely, ready to go, I was insanely excited for this race! We'd made a couple of setup changes from the race yesterday and thanks to David's wizardry, the engine was sounding sweet as a nut!

The lights went out and away we were away. This time, although I lit that solitary rear wheel up like mad once again, I managed a much better start, meaning that as we headed into turn one, I was right on the heels of the car in front. I was hoping with the engine now running much smoother that we might be able to keep up with him, and hopefully even challenge him for position. It took a couple of laps to get the gist of things, but I throughout these laps, I was able to keep right on his bumper, and eventually started pressuring him and making a couple of moves. He clearly had the brakes on me as I was still struggling, but there were a couple of points around the track where I was slightly faster than he was, so overall we were very well matched! On a number of occasions, I was able to get a good run on him through the last part of the lap, before slipstreaming past him down the start / finish straight and into turn one, for him to just do the opposite and get a good run on me through the first complex and slipstream me down towards Tower. We tussled for position like this for the whole race, for him to just pip me across the line. I was annoyed that I wasn't able to get him, but what a race it was! I'm sure Dad didn't get much a feel for it on the pit wall, and I'm sure Bex didn't think much of it from her vantage point at turn one, but in the cockpit, it was absolutely cracking! We even shared a very respectful thumbs up between one another through the back end of the track. Back in Parc Ferme and straight away there were handshakes and congratulations between us – if this was what the racing was going to be like in this formula, then this was without a doubt the right call!

Lewis: "Same again in an hour?"

Ayrton: "Absolutely, see you there! I'm going to have you this time though".

We headed back to the paddock after the obligatory weighing of the cars and took a well-deserved drink of water. Overall, all three of us were absolutely dead chuffed with the performance in that race! Very impressive from flag to flag, and we couldn't wait for the next race.

It's at this point that I feel I have missed out a very big part of the culture in the Mazda-Sevens. The formula is run by the 750 Motor Club, who do a brilliant job putting everything on, and maintaining the time at the meeting so no one start running late, and everyone gets all of their races in. However, as part of that, each formula seems to have a team who kind-of "runs" things day to day while you're at the meeting. The place where the trophies are handed out and stuff like that. In the Ma7da championship, that is done at Team Sellars Racing, and they have a delightful young gentleman called Dave (don't even bother trying to keep tabs of how many Dave's there are in this formula, you're wasting your breath!). Dave hands out the trophies at the end of the races, and comes around and checks up on people between the races. He is lovely, and always has a beaming smile. We get on very well with Dave, and he always makes a special effort to check how we are getting on, occasionally paying extra special attention to our times when we've had the odd successful meeting. At the end of the second race, Dave came up to us and wished massive congratulations for that performance, which was really lovely to see, and massively appreciated. It's always difficult coming into a new formula and not knowing anyone, but this meeting so far, everyone has been coming up and introducing themselves and that has been amazing!

One of Dave's pre-race rituals however is coming around to everyone and shaking their hand or giving them a little fist bump before heading out.

As we were sat in the holding area (with me 14th on the grid might I add, with my two race finishes), Dave wanders over and sees Lewis and I parked next to each other, shook both our hands, then stood back and loudly shouts "Another nice clean race please gents" before laughing and wandering over to the next competitor. That made me chuckle. My nerves were at a weekend-long low as we were sat ready to go out for the third race, and Dave's little comment, and how he had clearly been paying attention to our race, even though we were the opposite end of the track to where the "big action" was going on, just made me super sure that this was the formula for us!

We lined up on the grid for the third and final race of the weekend. I'd successfully cocked up every start so far, so this was my last chance to get it right. And guess what, I cocked it up again! Almost a carbon copy of the start in the second race, I got a lot of wheelspin, but managed to stick to the back of Lewis' car as we went through turn one. This race had the added excitement of being that bit further up because I'd finished every race that weekend, I was higher placed than people who'd done really well in the first race, then not finished the second, or vice versa. This all meant that as we headed into turn one, there were some almightily

ONE TYRE FIRE

fast cars around us! Fortunately, I did nothing stupid and let them get on with their race, so I could focus on mine.

Once we had cleared the gaggle of faster cars around us, Lewis and I basically fell into line, exactly like we were in the second race, earlier that day. Chopping and changing positions all the way around the track. I thought I might have him for good in a couple of places, but annoyingly, his car was just so good on the brakes – I couldn't work out how he was doing it! While I was hard on the anchors and going down the gears, he was still on the throttle, braking massively later than I was, but still ending up doing the same speed through the corner, how could he do it! All this meant that no matter how hard I kept pushing, I just couldn't hold him behind me. We were side by side as we started the last lap. I had him down the inside going into turn one, and managed to hold him behind as we exited the complex and onto the back straight. He was able to make a late dive for the inside and I did my best to hold it around the outside, but I was still on his bumper as we headed for the woodland section. Through sunny-in and sunny-out I thought I might be able to get a run on him into the last corner, but unfortunately, he was just about fast enough to keep my behind as we crossed the line. Another chequered flag and another outstanding race from inside the cockpit! It had been a tough weekend with some troubles along the way, but I had absolutely loved every minute of it! If this is what this formula was going to promise more of every time we went out, then this was without a doubt the right call for us!

Once again, we shook hands in Parc Ferme and shared a couple of laughs with the other drivers, before heading back to the paddock to pack up and get ready for the long drive home.

As is customary in the Ma7da championship, there is an awards ceremony at the end of the day, giving out the podium trophies for the meeting, thanking everyone and giving the odd shout-out here and there. It was lovely to get a little shout out as one of the rookies competing this weekend, even if our performance hadn't been particularly impressive on the timing screens. We were beyond thrilled with the results we had achieved, and couldn't wait to do it all over again for the next meeting at Anglesey.

If you had told me back when Ross and I discussed buying a couple of cars, way back at the final meeting of 2022, that at the next meeting I would be out with these guys in a car we built ourselves, and we put the whole thing together in 61 days AND on top of all of that, we managed to finish every race of the weekend, I would have called you mad. I don't think there was anyone in the paddock, in our friend groups, following on Facebook or anywhere else that would have gone "building a car in 61 days and racing it, while still working a full-time job, yeah that's doable!". Of everyone at the Ma7da championship who we explained our intentions to, I don't think one of them said "Yep, that's easily doable, not a problem". But nonetheless, we did it. Against all the odds, we managed the unimaginable.

The first meeting of the year was a fantastic weekend through and through, and I cannot ever thank everyone who helped us along the way enough. Should this collection of words and pages ever come to being an actual book, then it shall be dedicated to the good men and women of my family for helping make this all achievable! My dad for the countless hours he spent with me down the garage putting the car together, funnily enough I don't think the payment of tea and biscuits will quite cover it. My Mum for allowing me to steal all of Dad's time for the past two months. And of course, my amazing fiancée, Bex! We discussed this project late in 2022, that if it was to all come together as we hoped, I would be completely unavailable for those two months, but if it then all worked out, I'd then not need to spend hours and hours down the garage keeping the car together between meetings, and she was absolutely brilliant, supporting me the whole way. Plus, that journey to Croft on her own? Madness!

CHAPTER 12 – "AAAAAND BREATHE!"

Date: 18/04/2023

Time: 18:00

Location: The Garage

"It's over, we made it!"

As I open the garage up for the first time since the weekend (yesterday was my birthday so we went away for the night to get away and relax after the busy couple of months), the memories of the weekend come flooding back and I am filled with joy at the whole experience again. Of course, however, this is racing we are talking about, so no matter how amazing a meeting may be, you know there are always improvements that can, and need to, be made. Therefore, although thrilled at our performance, a large amount of the journey home in the van was spent discussing what needs to be done to make the car faster. We were ok on the weekend, but forget the sentimentality for a moment and you can quickly realise that we essentially finished last in every race – not so good when you think of it like that is it!

Therefore, what did we need to change? Firstly, the brakes – something needed to be done with the brakes. Discs, pads, whatever it was that needed changing, they needed changing. Along with the brakes was a small list of other things that needed sorting…

- Bonnet and nose need tidying up.
- Fix the alternator.
- Check for head gasket damage.
- Fit thermostat
- Weld leak in exhaust.
- Sort leaking half shafts.
- Breather for oil catch can
- Strip and check diff.

…and this was only a very small highlight of the full list. "But I thought the car was working fine?". Yes, technically the car was working fine, but "fine" and "perfectly" are two different things. The car was working well enough to keep finishing races and gaining pace, it wasn't working well enough to start making some sizable leaps up the grid, and as we had about 4 weeks between now and the next meeting, those leaps are what we need to start chasing. We had a small leak from the half shafts, the engine temperature was being a little funny at times, the exhaust was leaking a little making it slightly louder than it should be – those kind of things. You don't care about them at the track because they aren't stopping you from getting out, but they're the kind of thing that can bite you in the ass if you don't sort them.

So, the next few weeks were spent working through the new job list we had made on the whiteboard. One thing you need to know about job lists on racing cars, they are never empty. You clear the list, then you just find more things that need attention, but aren't important enough to need to go on the first list. When you then clear that list you make another, then another, and by the time you've cleared that list, you've either crashed the car and then fill the whiteboard with jobs to fix it, or it's the winter break and you then fill the whiteboard again with jobs to do over the winter that you haven't had time to do over the season. Then the new season starts again and you go through it all again. Racing is basically just writing stuff on the whiteboard and rubbing it off until you retire, should you choose to do something so silly!

The main thing as mentioned already was that the brakes needed improving. I had bought the rear brakes from Dave Boucher, and the front brakes are standard Mk3/4/5 Ford Cortina, so all the parts are available off the shelf. I wasn't sure what to get so I just bought fast road performance bits. Our cars weigh in at 665kg with the driver onboard, so these brakes don't need to work too hard. Go too racey on the pads and discs and you'll never switch them on, go too gentle and they won't stop the car quickly enough. I think I went a little too racey with my choice of front pads, and a little too gentle on the discs to go with them, and I don't think they matched nicely with the rears. So overall, I was struggling to get them all to work together and they came alive at different temperatures, which also didn't help.

My solution was a set of new brake discs on the front, nice racey ones! And to go with this, a new set of pads all around, but the same make and material for all of them so I could guarantee they will warm up and work evenly together. As well as this, I was struggling to get used to how much travel I had on the pedal, so I adjusted the pedal ratio and fitted a new set of master cylinders to help give a more positive feel. After changing everything over and bleeding the system, the pedal felt much nicer on the foot than it had, so I was feeling confident that that was fixed.

As mentioned, we also struggled with over (and under) heating the engine. Our nose solution, although just about acceptable to get us out there, wasn't letting enough air through the radiator, and we think that was the reason the engine was getting hot. We also forewent fitting the thermostat in the water system, which we think might have been causing us other issues, so we fitted a new one along with the changes to the nose to hopefully fix both problems. This should allow much more air through the radiator, as well as giving a variable flow of water through the cooling system, meaning the engine can stay at a much more suitable temperature.

The 4-week break was over before we knew it, and although there had been a number of big leaps on the car, a good engineer will always want to make further adjustments. Nonetheless, we'd managed to improve the most important bits, and had a good go at improving some of the more minor bits. I think the biggest thing that I was desperate to fix, but simply didn't have the time for was the improvement to the nose. I simply didn't get the positioning quite right here, which left the front end look like some kind of deep-sea fish with its mouth wide open – it looked stupid! No matter, it would do, and if nothing else, it would definitely force plenty of air through the radiator. We were heading for North Wales in May; I certainly wasn't expecting any warm weather there!

As it turned out, and not for the first time this year, I was wrong.

CHAPTER 13 – WHO'D'VE GUESSED, ANOTHER LONG JOURNEY!

Date: 12/05/2023

Time: 15:30

Location: Sainsbury's Car Park, Exeter

There was a lot playing on my mind for this weekend. The car had been relatively successful, in our minds, for the first meeting at Croft, as our expectations were very low. Finishing all three races, regardless of where we finished was a win in our books for a car thrown together in under two months with nothing more than grit, determination, and Party Rings! However, all this meant that we needed to go further forward this weekend. Rookie meeting over and done with now, we needed to start showing some improvements. If nothing else, I needed to show myself that the changes that had been made to the car over the last month were worthwhile. We had about the same number of entries for Anglesey as we had for Croft, so to me, finishing higher than we had at the first meeting, and showing some promise against the other cars would be a successful outing – anything else is a bonus!

Another thing playing on my mind was that this was my first meeting (ever, might I just add) that I had been to without Dad there. Lee Rogers has been racing considerably longer than I have been alive. He's been successful in Short Circuit Hot Rods and Stock Rods, before making the leap to Pickup Truck Racing, where he has been highly competitive for a number of years, in a discipline littered with very high budget teams. Little ol' Team Rogers Racing, turning up every weekend with their trusty van and trailer, we really are very small fish, in one hell of a pond! Because of this, and especially so over the past few years, racing has mainly been the story of Dad and I trapsing across the UK, running the show on our own. If he was racing, I was there as crew, and if I was racing, he was there as crew. This weekend unfortunately coincided with a holiday that he and my Mum had planned months in advance, meaning this would be the first time that he wasn't there when I was away racing. I knew what I was doing, so I had no concerns there, but it didn't half feel odd not having him there to rattle ideas off when we're trying to make the car faster.

Fortunately, however, Bex was dead keen for a weekend away, and a long-standing friend of mine, Stan, was also up for a bit of a jolly. And just to top off the cake, and old collegemate of mine and Stan's, Jordy, lived not too far away from Anglesey, so said he would come and meet us there for the weekend too – lovely!

Bex and I had both gotten the Friday afternoon off with the intentions of getting the best leap on the Friday traffic as possible, but Stan wasn't as flush with annual leave as we were, which limited us to picking him up from the local supermarket car park near his work, as finished up for the day. We were all loaded up and on the road shortly after 15:30 for the "short" journey up to Anglesey. The sat-nav read that it was going to be the best part of a 6-hour journey, and that didn't include any inevitable diversions for Friday night traffic.

We made some cracking time up to North Wales, passing the hours chatting bollocks and generally catching up. Also, learning that Stan had developed a liking for "nice pylons". Nope, I didn't get it either. He did assure us however that it was just electrical pylons and no double-entendres though! Fortunately, we were able to make the majority of the journey without encountering too much traffic. The only struggle we had was the sat-nav diverting us off the motorway to take some horrible backroads not too far from Oulton Park. One common topic that made numerous appearances however was whether or not young Jordy was going to turn up the next morning. One thing you need to know about Jordy is that he either doesn't turn up for most things, or turns up so late that he might as well not have. I was confident that my good mate of many years wouldn't let me down as he knew how excited we all were to catch up, but both Bex and Stan were both adamantly confident that he was going to bail. The conversations went on for mile after mile after mile with both sides of the fence arguing their certainty of their point, tooth and nail. Eventually, it was decided to "make it interesting", and we did the now obligatory betting of ice-creams on the outcome. One thing you need to know, here at Team Rogers Racing, when buying the journey home ice-creams is bet on, you know it's serious! Dad and Brian used to have "50p bets", but with inflation over the years, I've opted to introduce "Ice cream bets" instead.

We pulled into the circuit at God-knows-what o'clock and managed to find a place to land the van. Anglesey is one of the few circuits in the UK that Team Rogers had never been to before, so it was difficult getting your bearings of somewhere when it is pitch-black, and you've just spent the best part of 7 hours travelling up in the van, but we managed.

Saturday – Qualifying and Race 1 (and the confirmation of who would be buying the ice creams!)

Daylight broke at what we quickly realised was one of the most beautiful circuits in the UK. It was a glorious day with not a cloud in the sky all day long, and barely any wind! Given that the circuit is right next to the sea, and a MASSIVE crash at turn 2 would put you in the drink, for there to be no bone-chilling gale, we thought was a miracle! The troops all got up fairly early Saturday morning as qualifying was on at 9:20 and we still needed to unload, prep the car and setup our living quarters for the weekend. The others would claim it wasn't the case, but I felt an edge of tension in the air that morning – would Jordy turn up or not! Those two had ripped into me for hours last night, and all I wanted right at that moment was for him to pull up so I could give him a nice big hug and gloat!

We had no scrutineering this weekend, which was nice as it meant we had just that little bit more time to get everything ready on the car. I had made a couple of changes to the setup on the car in preparation for the weekend, but otherwise it was fairly similar to how we had it at Croft (other than everything we had changed of course). The main thing that I needed to get going were the brakes. We had no practice or testing session where I could focus on getting them dialled in, so annoyingly I knew I had to sacrifice qualifying to make sure the brakes we absolutely cooking for the race later today. One thing you need to know about this formula – qualifying is key! The racing is very close with these guys, which means it is hard work to push your way through the grid; therefore, you need a cracking qualifying to make sure you are up there for the races. Annoyingly however, we had to simply bite the bullet this weekend!

Ring ring

"Yep mate, I am about 10 minutes away".

Amazing! Regardless of the outcome of the racing, now it was going to be a good weekend! Yes, I had won the bet, and I can assure you now, I was not a gracious winner!

Qualifying beckoned and not before long, we were sat in the holding area ready to go out. As I mentioned, I'd never been here before, never walked the track and only put in a handful of laps on the Xbox to work out which way the track went – at least I had been to Croft a couple of times so kind of knew what I was doing. The holding area at Anglesey is right as you lead onto the start / finish line, so you essentially start a "flying" lap right off the bat – does at least give you a chance to get your eye in for a full lap, and turn one doesn't take you by surprise! Knowing I needed to get the brakes working, and learn the track, I quickly found some free space with a couple of cars shortly ahead of me and started dialling everything in. One thing it took me only a lap or so to work out, was that the new brakes were absolutely amazing! I got a little too excited here and there, with a large amount of locked wheels as the session went on, but I was feeling confident. Unfortunately, due to the size of the International circuit here, we couldn't get a massive amount of laps in before the session was finished. This meant by the time I had the brakes somewhere suitable, and had started getting my eye in for the track, I had only got a couple of "fast" laps to my name. This meant that I had qualified 16th of 18 for both races. No matter, I was fairly happy with the car and was starting to get the gist of the track – bring on race 1!

Fortunately, the car didn't need much work between qualifying and race 1, a simple tyre pressure check and a top-up of fuel and she was good to go. This gave us all a chance to catch up and enjoy the sunshine. Some of us even had a little nap and needed waking up by the driver as we were called to the holding area for the race.

Sat in the holding area ready for the race, and almost on cue, Dave walks over and once again tells Lewis (who I'd qualified right next to once again) and I to play nicely out there!

Because you pull straight out of holding and onto the grid, being at the back is especially bad, as there is no time to warm the car up for the race, so I did my best in the space I had, and dutifully took my spot on the grid. Once again, I wasn't sure on the revs to pull at the start, other than knowing it needed to be considerably lower than before!

The lights went out, and guess which tosser once again cocked up the launch! No matter, much like the last couple of races at Croft, although I had a bad start, it wasn't disastrous and I was quickly on the heels of the cars in front. Turn one off the line is almost a "nothing corner" as you aren't carrying enough speed to need to do anything – turn 2 however is a different story! In our little kit-cars, it feels like you can go 20-wide, and some people certainly gave it their best to do so. We managed to tuck in nice and tight, and I thought make up some good positions. It was at this point that I quickly realised that tucking in super tight at turn 2 on the first lap is possibly the silliest thing you can do at Anglesey, as this just means you are carrying no momentum by the time you get to the end of the straight and into Rocket. From here on in however, it was a different story. There was a small gaggle of us towards the back of the grid, comfortably filling out positions 9 to 17, and I don't think there was a lap from flag to flag where those positions stayed as they were. Some truly amazing battles throughout the pack for the whole race. A personal highlight of mine, if you don't mind me tooting my own trumpet, was a spectacular double overtake down the inside of Matt Graux and Peter Wood into the final corner. I was so chuffed with that move that I very nearly locked up the brakes altogether and ploughed into the run-off area. Fortunately, I was able to hold it and press on through the pack, but I think the grin on my face was visible from the side of the track!

As the race continued on, and we entered the final couple of laps, I had my eyes burning a hole in the back of Imran Khan's Mazda 787B liveried car. He'd been a few too many lengths in front of me for a lap or so at this point, but by now I was closing in and forcing the odd mistake. I had no clue which position I was in at this point, but I was desperate to tick one more place off the list. I was trying everything to sneak down the inside here or outside there, but he put up a spectacular fight! I was struggling for straight-line speed compared to him, and he was unable to match what I was doing through the twisties, so over a lap we were very well matched. The "Final Lap" board was shown and I was right on his bumper as we crossed the line. I knew I only had a couple of places I could make a move. I couldn't carry the speed down the straight to warrant making a move into 1 or 2, as he would simply pull back the time down the next straight. If I made a VERY ballsy move into Rocket, I might be able to pull away enough through the corners at the top of the hill before he closed back on the International Loop – it was a very tricky one to judge! I opted to try and make the move into Rocket under the heavy braking zone. My car was absolutely electric on the brakes this weekend with the changes made, and I was confident I could do it, I just needed to hold onto him down the straight. Coming into Rocket and although I couldn't make the move, I was right up behind him. He managed a good exit from all of the proceeding corners and I thought that was it. Fortunately, however, he slightly fumbled the exit from the hairpin heading down towards the last corner and I saw my chance. I pulled alongside him and we had a drag-race into the last corner. I knew I could have him on the brakes, I just needed to ensure I could hold it through the tight final corner. On the brakes and I managed to get half a length in front of him, but as we turned into the corner side-by-side, the back end of my car stepped out slightly and I was forced to wrestle it back into shape as we emerged towards the chequered flag. The gap was 2 tenths of a second between us as we crossed the line, and unfortunately, the #79 machine was the trailing car of the two. Gutted that I hadn't managed to pull the move off, but I was absolutely ecstatic at the race we'd just had! Absolutely amazing, and still at this point I didn't know where I was. Honestly though, I didn't really care – you go racing for the enjoyment of the sport, not the numbers and stats at the end.

That being said, as I pulled back into the paddock, with the whole team running over, hugging and congratulating me on my FIRST TOP 10 FINISH, I was absolutely over the moon! Not only had we had a phenomenal race, but to score my best ever finish, and first ever top 10, what a result that was! The other teams must have looked over and thought we had gone mad, celebrating like crazy for a tenth-place finish, but I didn't care what they thought, we were buzzing!

Once the joy of the race had died down slightly (not that it died down completely for a good couple of weeks), we went about our checks on the car. I had noticed the voltmeter was showing about 17/18V towards the end of the race (it should be about 14.5V), but I just blocked it out of my head for the last few laps. We had a spare alternator in the van, it'll probably be fine, I thought! Once the car had cooled off, I swapped the alternators over, made a couple of small setup changes to the car, and sat down for a well earnt cider.

The weather on Saturday had been amazing all day long, with most of us getting slightly sunburnt as the hours drew on. Therefore, we decided to have a nice evening walk around the track, so the others could get a feel for the place, and I could try and learn a bit more before the second race the following day.

Sunday – Race 2

When we awoke Sunday morning, if the giant "Anglesey" sign hadn't been within view of our camp, you could have assumed that we had gone to a completely different track! Gone were the clear skies and beautiful sunshine, replaced with cloud and some light drizzle – ahh, good old Welsh weather!

We had nothing that needed doing to the car that morning as I had gone to the effort of sorting it the night before. Therefore, it was a nice, chilled morning before the second, and final, race of the weekend at 11:00. I was considering what to do with the setup, where normally Dad and I would discuss what to do in conditions like these, before he would normally call me one of his cute pet-names, like "Ratbag" or "Little Princess" and tell me to just go out there and get my head down – ahh, a father's love, you can't hack it, can you!

I opted to try a small tweak to the crossweight to make the car a bit more stable on the rear and (hopefully) eliminate some of the loose conditions that I was fighting the day before.

We lined up for the final start of the weekend and for the first time this year, I made a half-decent start! Finally getting to grips with the right amount of revs to pull, I didn't get too much wheelspin and was able to keep up with the cars in front. This race was somewhat different to that of yesterday's, more than likely because of the drizzle, people were being a bit more cautious, and our little convoy followed line-astern for a full lap or so.

Heading into Rocket on lap 2, at one of the fastest points on the track, well up towards the top end of 4th gear, Daniel Sibbons and Dave Mason had a small coming together, which resulted in Daniel spinning off and collecting the barriers, hard. Fortunately, he was relatively fine, and got out of the car, but he had been badly winded and slightly injured from the crash. His car had also taken some serious damage too. This whole incident resulted in a safety car, which turned into a red flag and a restart.

The lights went out once again, and I made another good getaway. Once we'd made it through the first couple of corners, the tussling from the first race began in earnest once again, with our little gaggle at the rear of the grid chopping and changing positions corner to corner. We had some spectacular racing with everyone involved, but annoyingly ended up chasing Imran once again towards the end of the race. This time however, he had managed to pull a large number of car lengths on us, and by the time I made it free of the pack,

I wasn't able to mount an attack on him for 10th place. I crossed the line in what I thought was another very well-deserved finish. 5/5 finishes for the year - I was dead chuffed with that! There were a few things I wanted to work on before the next meeting out at Mallory Park, but for now, I was happy with the results of the weekend, and glad to be moving up in the grid. Fingers crossed we can do that some more next time!

For now, though, I am going to enjoy this ice cream on the way home.

CHAPTER 14 – UPGRADES PEOPLE, UPGRADES!

Date: 16/05/2023

Time: 16:30

Location: The Garage

Much like after the meeting at Croft, we had a 4-week break between Anglesey and our next meeting at Mallory Park. We'd taken no damage, and the car was running fairly well all weekend once more, so I took it upon myself to find somethings that probably didn't need doing!

It will come as no surprise, that although there was nothing that "needed" doing on the car, the list of "nice-to-haves" quickly filled the whiteboard. One thing that I was keen to work on was the rear-end stability of the car. It was something that I was struggling with all weekend, and knew that we were giving away heaps of time going through the faster corners compared to our competitors. I had also noticed that there was a small break forming between us and the cars in front between gears. To get the car ready for Croft (and due to ol' lanky legs here), I had had to modify a standard gearstick so I could actually reach the stick and change gears. This combined to making the throw between them excessively long. Therefore, a short-shift kit was definitely one to add to the list! The final "big one" that really wanted doing was a foam seat-infill – one of those fancy moulded things. We'd never needed to do one of those before, as all of the seats we have run in the past have come with their own padding to squeeze the driver into place; this seat however was a little big for me with no padding, and through the faster corners, I could feel myself sliding from one side of the seat to the other. Another shopping spree later and after a couple of days, another care package of shiny bits turned up on our front door. However, this was not the extent of the modifications we were undertaking before Mallory.

Back in 2020, Dad and I had put together a fairly simple tyre rack to mount to the front of the trailer. Back then, it was done to house the spare wheels for the Mallock, along with a fleet of other items. Since then, however, it has spent most of its time rusting away in the corner of the workshop, and we thought something needed doing about that!

One thing we had realised was that taking the most space in the van was the spare tyres and the cans of fuel that we needed for the weekend. Could we make a little attachment for our rack to house the tyres we were taking, but also the cans of fuel so they didn't need to live in the van? A quick mock-up and some CAD design later, and a "do it yourself" trailer storage box turned up. An evening's welding, painting and fitting later and we had ourselves a shiny tyre rack, appropriately adorning various "Team Rogers Racing" logos – it looked epic if I do say so myself!

So, there we had it. The car had been improved, the trailer had been improved, and Dad had passed on his immortal words of wisdom of the impending track, "whatever you do, just try and miss the big wet bit in the middle of the circuit"! Sounds like we were ready for Mallory!

CHAPTER 15 – "WELL DAMN, WASN'T EXPECTING THAT!"

Date: 10/06/2023

Time: 14:30

Location: Outside the garage

ONE TYRE FIRE

Race weekend is once again upon us! This is our first single-day event of the season, another double-header, like Anglesey was, but this time everything is covered in the one day. All this meant that we were leaving at the highly unusual time of half 2 in the afternoon on a Saturday of all things! For this weekend, we were also taking Mum and Dad's motorhome, instead of our trusty race-van. Mum, Dad, Bex and I were all packed up and hitting the road this time – the first meeting of the year that Mum has been to, no doubt her nerves are higher than mine!

We got to Mallory Park in the early evening, the sun was still shining and the paddock was bustling with activity. It was an early start in the morning, so everyone was getting there the night before in preparation. We'd been to Mallory a number of times in the past, but when Dad is here with the Pickups, they normally race on the oval. I wasn't quite sure what to make of the track as we walked the 1.35-mile layout, it's very fast, but the layout is simple; 4 corners, three rights with one left. Sounds easy enough doesn't it! As it turns out, I really enjoyed this track, and despite it sounding simple enough, it is far from it.

Morning came and we went about our final checks before qualifying. I wasn't sure what to aim for here. I'd never driven the track, but it was a fairly simple and short layout, meaning I should be able to get plenty of laps in over the 15-minute session. We also had some very special guests this weekend too – Ross, Kelly and their daughter, Margot had made the journey up in the morning to support us, and to give Ross and chance to see the cars he'd be racing against soon, in the flesh.

The Tannoy came alive and we were called to the holding area for qualifying – too late for any last-minute changes now; we had what we had. The sun was beating down on the track hard, and even though it was still very early in the day, I was glad to be sat in an open-top car! As we pulled onto the track, I intended to use the first couple of laps to get my eye in for the track, before trying to find someone to latch onto and get a good slipstream off. As luck would have it, a very rapid Ben Powney came past me after a handful of laps, and I then used the next 10 or so laps to follow him and learn what he was doing. On lap 13, Ben pulled to the side of the track, along with a number of other drivers who had pushed their tyres a little too hard in these hot conditions, releasing me to put some laps in on my own. As it turned out, lap 14 was then my fastest of the session. Eventually, the chequered flag came out and we made our way back to the pits. I'd felt really comfortable out on track, and was really loving the layout! Although simple enough, the nature of the circuit leaves masses of time out there for the driver to find, should he or she have enough confidence to go looking.

I pulled into our awning after the session, feeling good. Dad got back from pit lane at about the same time and said that we had looked really quick, which was a bit of a confidence boost to add to the weekend too. It's always one thing to feel fast in the car, but you can't really judge your pace when you're on your own, for Dad to think we were going quickly against the other cars was a big win to start the day off with. It was at this moment that a very excited Dave walked over to our awning with his beaming smile as always! "Congratulations mate, that was cracking, good job!" I thanked him, and asked why he was congratulating me. At this point, we'd not seen a timing sheet, so had no idea where we had qualified. "Don't you know where you qualified?" Dave asked. I said that I didn't, funnily enough, I'd been a little busy the last 15 minutes to check the timing screen. He eventually relented and confirmed that we had indeed been the 6th fastest car on the track! 6th fastest, I couldn't believe it! I knew the car had felt better than it had at Anglesey, but that was a huge leap forward on the grid and we were over the moon. He congratulated us again before heading off to speak with some other drivers. Dad and I got a moment of celebration between us before the rest of the team got back and started congratulating me too. Absolutely cracking, I could not believe it – still can't believe it now! To make such a leap forward in the timings was a big deal for us as every other qualifying session of the year we had essentially qualified at the back – 6th was a hell of a step up!

Right then, don't let it get to your head, we still had two races to get through, you can't pop the champagne after qualifying! We got on with the prep for the race, the usual stuff, tyres, fuel and whatnot and opted as the car was feeling really good, to leave the setup exactly as it was. It was really drivable around the fast corners here, with only a mere hint of understeer when you start pushing a little too hard – I was happy with that! One thing that's been a struggle all year is getting used to the different way to set the car up. We are used to cars with much more power, big sticky slick tyres, and limited slip diffs. Normally I would set a car up for a little bit of slip on the rear wheels, and drive the car with the loud pedal, but we were quickly realising that you just can't drive these cars like that (well, I can't at least!). Momentum is key, and putting the car into a big slide is just time you are giving away, and the grid is so competitive, any time you are giving away could be a position or even more than you are losing.

We were called to the holding area for Race 1, and I was chuckling to myself at the shock on the other drivers faces as they saw me drastically out of position for the grid. I also couldn't quite believe that I was lined up alongside the championship leader, when normally this season I've not even been able to see his car as we line up on the grid! Due to the nature of the circuit here at Mallory, this is one of the places where we actually get a suitable amount of time to warm the tyres and brakes up on the way to the grid, which I was dead chuffed about! We pulled up to our boxes on the grid, and the lights came on. I had spent many an evening going through people's onboard footage leading up to this meeting to make sure I would get the best start possible. I'd worked out how many revs the other drivers were pulling so I could do my best to match it. The lights went out, and I made a cracking start! As we exited turn one, I was right on the heels of the leaders, even so much so that I was trying for a move for 5th place into the hairpin! Unfortunately, Martin Shelton got a cracking run on me through the final corner, and was able to slip past me into the first corner. I was able to hang on to the back of the leading car train, and positions were chopping and changing almost every corner. Jonathan Lisseter had dropped down a couple of positions from the start, and was battling it out with Simon Cort and myself, with David Bowen hot on our heels behind. I was doing my best to follow what Jonathan was doing, but annoyingly he was able to slip past Simon into the hairpin and make a speedy getaway. I tried for a few laps after this to make a move on Simon, but he defended exceptionally well and I was unable to make a move past him. As the race drew towards its dying laps, I made a bold move down the inside of him into the hairpin, but annoyingly locked up and went wide, allowing Simon to escape my clutches, and also allowing David Bowen through. Fortunately, my car was still showing some exceptional pace in the final few laps of the race, and it wasn't long before I was right on David's bumper once again. The changes we'd made to the brakes before the Anglesey meeting were definitely showing their worth here! With about 3 laps to go, two of the cars in the leading pack had mechanical troubles and pulled off the track, moving us a little higher up the order. I hadn't been able to keep track of the position we were in by this point, and firmly had my eyes locked on the rear bumper of David's #25 car!

The last lap board was held at the side of the track, and I knew that time was running thin, this was it now, if we were making a move, it had to be done! We started the final lap nearly side by side after I got a good run out of the last corner, but David was able to cover the inside as we entered into turn 1. I could tell that his tyres were starting to get a little too hot as I could see his car slipping and sliding, so I hoped I could get a good run out of the corner and down the inside into turn 2. My premonition came true absolutely perfectly, and I was able to get a good run on him into the next corner, and down the inside. Annoyingly, with the setup we were running on my car, the understeer I had briefly experienced in qualifying was hitting hard as we came into turn 2 side by side. Just about able to wrestle the car through the corner, I got a big kick of oversteer as I hit the marbles on the exit of the corner and David was able to slip back through again. Not deterred, I held myself on the inside into the hairpin and braked as late as I dared! Now I was in front, but David got a much better run out of the hairpin and into the final corner – it was a drag race to the line! I opted for the tighter line through the final corner, hoping the steeper slope at the apex would help propel me towards the finish line. We crossed the line half a car length between us, #79 leading #25!

As I pulled back into the pits I was still none the wiser to where I'd finished, but I was absolutely beaming! What a race that was, and to snatch that final position across the line, I couldn't be happier with the result! As it turned out, we'd finished in 6th place after all of the chopping and changing, aided by the couple of cars not finishing the race too. Much like in qualifying, I simply could not believe it, a new best finishing result for me, and we were really showing some brilliant pace in the car now. Still not quite fast enough to threaten the leading pack, but enough to show some intent if nothing else!

We had a couple of hours break between races 1 and 2, and fortunately there was once again nothing that needed doing to the car. A quick wipe down, bolt check, level check and top it off with fuel and we were ready to go.

As we pulled up to the grid for the final race of the weekend, I was eager to get going. Race 1 had proven what I needed to do to nail the starts, the car was absolutely singing, and I couldn't wait to see what the final race would bring. The lights went out and another very good start from us, but out of nowhere came the purple #7 car of Daniel Cort, flying past me and a number of other drivers in the process! He must've made 4 places before turn 1, no idea how he did that! We headed into the first corner as an 18 strong cluster of Mazda-sevens, inches between each car, first through to last. I exited the corner chasing down Sam McKee (in the car Imran was driving at Anglesey), with Lucas Batt right on my tail. As we headed for turn 2, Lucas made a dive down the inside of me, but opted to bail out. The three of us chased for a couple of laps until Lucas finally made the move stick on me down into the hairpin, only for me to snatch it back a couple of laps later in the same place, around the outside. As luck would have it, this move also managed to sneak me down the inside of Sam into the final corner to have both positions by the time we crossed the start line. I was expecting to have the both of them baring down on me in no time, so I got my head down and focused on trying to break a gap. Fortunately, I was able to do so, and a few corners later I had a bit of breathing space behind me. Daniel Cort had made a break for it by this time and was absolutely miles clear of me, with the pack of the 6 leaders well clear of him too. It's common knowledge in this formula, that if you are running around on your own, it's very unlikely that you are going to be able to catch the cars in front, as a pack can slipstream each other and increase its pace, so I was fairly confident that it was unlikely I would progress any further up the grid.

Lap 9

I'd spent the last 4/5 laps on my own, putting in qualifying lap after qualifying lap, and now I was right on the tail of Daniel. My car clearly had good pace around here, and I was doing everything I could to try and catch him up, and amazingly, it was working! I had a good run through turn 2 and made an almighty lunge down the inside of him into the hairpin! Once again proving how good this car was on the brakes, I was through and gone by the next corner with the leading pack a speck at the end of the next straight. "No chance" I thought….."but hey, what the hell, I've come this far, let's see how close I can get!". I was using the fast right hander of turn 2 to gauge how close I was getting to the leading pack, and lap by lap, I could tell that I was reeling them in! I couldn't believe it, I knew I had good pace this weekend, but good enough to reel in the leaders all on my own?

Surely not! Lap 13 came and I was getting well within the point of being able to start showing my intentions to the leaders. I thought at this point that just latching onto the back of them is the best thing I could do at this point, try and force an error and make my way further up the grid. As we piled into the hairpin, now 7 cars strong, I was right in the mixing. I knew the pace I had going into the hairpin was one of the strongest, and I wanted to capitalise.

Lap 14

I had a terrific run through turn 2 and into the hairpin. All 6 of the leaders had gone defensive, 3 rows of 2 from first to sixth, with me in seventh, on my own on the outside. There was a clear gap and we were entering my favourite corner! I didn't hesitate to throw the car down the outside on the brakes, and quickly slipped past Martin Shelton and Anthony Ridd.

It was at this point that the racing gods threw down the gauntlet.

Unfortunately, the two cars on my inside had a small coming together, throwing Martin to the outside of the corner. If I had held back just one more corner, I would have watched it all happen in front of me and pick up the pieces. I had however made the bold call to go for the move down the outside. This resulted in Martin, unable to do anything about it, leaping into the side of my car, putting me parked at the side of the track – everything I had worked towards lost in the blink of an eye! That is, however, racing. Unfortunately, you are just in the wrong place at the wrong time sometimes.

This was not the end of the race though. The engine was still running, and to the best of my knowledge, the car wasn't bent, so as quickly as I could, I got going again and re-began my pursuit. Annoyingly, the cars following behind me were all close enough that there wasn't a safe place for me

to pull out until I was down in 12th place. So, the promising top 10 finish was now lying in tatters. That being said however, I was still able to bring the car home for the final few laps and cross the finish line. By the time I had caught back to the car in front of me, I was running out of laps to push much further forward, and he did a spectacular job of defending, so I was unable to make it past.

No matter though. Aside from the disappointment of the result in the second race, I was still very pleased with the pace of both me, and the car all weekend (even though my face and body language wouldn't show it for a good few hours). We had

gone to Mallory with 10th being the best finish I'd achieved this year, and basically last being the best I had qualified, and I had smashed both of those results out of the park! To add to that, apparently, I had held the fastest lap briefly during the second race, and when the chequered flag flew, I had the third fastest lap of the race overall. These are all monumental landmarks that we had to celebrate given that only 2 meetings previously, we were fighting hard (and failing, might I add) to not be last – to now be threatening the leaders, who consist of multiple champions, is an absolutely astonishing feat! Let alone, all of this in a car that 6 months ago, was a pile of 25mm square box section in Alan Coller's workshop. Once I had come to terms with all of this, the remainder of the journey home was much more enjoyable. We were all very proud of what we had achieved and were excited for the next meeting out. Another track I have never driven before, but this is one I was desperately looking forward to, Cadwell Park.

CHAPTER 16 – "UMMM, WHAT DO WE DO NOW?"

Date: 22/06/2023

Time: 17:30

Location: The Garage

The joy and woe of the weekend at Mallory had played in my mind. I had watched the onboard footage repeatedly and shown it to friends and family, who had all said they would have done the exact same thing if they were the ones driving. This made me feel much happier with my decision, but I just couldn't stop thinking about what might have happened if I had held back for just one more lap! Two of the cars in the leading 6 didn't finish the race due to mechanical troubles – could I have made it into the top 5? Was a podium on the cards?

A racing driver will always contemplate the "what if's" but what's done, is done, and nothing could be done to change that. I needed to move on, write it off as a learning experience, and grow from it.

The next meeting was Cadwell Park, I have been there once before, but never driven the track. A lot of friends had raved about how it was a brilliant track, and I had driven it on games over the years, and must admit that I was excited to drive the UK's version of the Nürburgring.

Although we had no damage from Mallory, the knock into the hairpin did give us a good excuse to go through the car with a fine-tooth comb, just in case something had bent somewhere on the car. We checked over every nook and cranny, but couldn't find anything untoward, which was a relief! As there was nothing fundamentally wrong with the car, there wasn't a lot that needed doing to it. The only part of the car causing concern was the gearstick. The poor design of the short-shift kit I had bought had caused some serious wear to the stick after just one meeting. For some reason, whoever made this kit thought it needed a plastic liner, rather than steel like Mazda had designed, and this plastic liner was nearly completely perished already. Fortunately, I am a design engineer, and know a fleet of people who love turning bar stock into swarf! A week or so later, I collected my brand-new stick, reimagined slightly with my own flourish here and there, just needing the finishing touch of some heat and a thorough twatting with a big hammer to finesse it into the right shape for my lanky physique. Straight away, this new stick was a massive improvement! No longer did it feel like the car was in neutral while being engaged in 4th at full chat.

Setup wise, we weren't really sure what the best cause of action was going to be. The car was very fast and very drivable at Mallory, but Cadwell Park and Mallory Park are two very different tracks! Mallory has 4 corners, 3 rights and 1 left. Cadwell has 17 corners, 11 rights and 6 lefts. However, despite this, we opted to leave the car as it was from Mallory. We knew it wasn't going to be correct, but we had to start somewhere, and this was at least a fast setup that I was used to.

CHAPTER 17 – "ARE YOU FEELING OK?"

Date: 07/07/2023

Time: 21:30

Location: Cadwell Park

Bex and I had left at about midday to make the 7-hour journey up to Cadwell Park. Once again, not a close one for us, but the sun was shining and we were excited! Mum and Dad are heading off on holiday straight from the track on Sunday night, so they were making their own way up in the motorhome, and as qualifying wasn't until about 11 the next day, they decided to come up the following morning. We had a paid practice first thing, which allowed me a better chance of getting my eye in around this tight and twisty track, so thought it was smarter to make the journey the day prior. By the time we got to the track and setup, we were more than ready for a beer and a gentle stroll around the circuit. Having been here before in 2020 with Dad, I remembered how hilly the track was, but I think it took Bex by surprise!

Saturday morning came around and we were called for the early practice session. The timings in the morning were a little tight as scrutineering was right after the session, so I hoped there were no troubles. Fortunately for us, it went down faultlessly and I was really starting to get my eye in around the complex 3.5-mile circuit. I recall making the argument that you could do 100 laps around this place and still find chunks of time the next time you went around! An amazing track it was, for sure, but my god was it tricky to work out the fastest way around - what I would have given for a fancy lap timer. Eventually, the 30-minute session was over, and the chequered flag came out. As I then proceeded to roll through the first corner, I immediately felt very unwell! Hastily making my way back to the paddock and into the queue for scrutineering, I leapt out of the car and made a scarper for the loos. Fortunately, I was fine after a couple of minutes and made my way back to the car, but when Bex caught up with me, she wasn't particularly confident in the colour I had turned. I'd been warned about the effect the track had on bringing on seasickness, but I didn't think I would have to worry about it; after all, I'd raced plenty of tracks before without any issues, why would this be any different. Fortunately, we flew through scrutineering with no troubles, and I made my way back to the van for a drink and some tablets. We also found some seasickness bands, which I quickly put on, and kept on for the rest of the weekend!

Following our return to the paddock, I went about checking over the car and topping off the fuel ready for qualifying. It wasn't long after this that Mum and Dad turned up, and Dad and I started work on a couple of small setup changes before eventually being called to the holding area. We had a fairly stiff, dry setup on the car, and were hoping that the adjustments we had made following the testing session would give me a little more confidence to start pushing harder. The whistle blew signalling to start engines and head out onto the track – too late for any more setup changes now, time to get your head down!

This is where things got a little...soggy.

As I pulled out of the holding area, I passed the marshals post and instantly we were driving in a full-blown monsoon. Not 10 seconds previously I had been sat in the car, ready to go out, with the sun beating down and not a drop of rain to be seen. Now, heading into the woodland section of the track, keeping the car pointed in the right direction was like wrestling a cougar while wearing mittens. The whole grid tried their best to go as fast as possible, but the conditions were absolutely appalling. Simply driving straight down the start line was a challenge, as the puddles that had appeared were catching the car and throwing it one way and another. It was a struggle to achieve full throttle without the back end trying to overtake the front, and add to this the complete lack of visibility, it was a huge challenge to keep the car pointing in the right direction! A number of the leaders quickly made their way past me, and I watched as most of them span out down the straights or off at the corners. Everyone fought valiantly to keep their cars pointing forwards, but after only 2 laps, the safety car was deployed to keep us at a reasonable pace, and bank the 3 laps we all needed to qualify for the races. Eventually, the red flag came out and we were all escorted back to the paddock, completely soaked through. Sods Law shone through shortly after, as almost as soon as we pulled into the paddock, the rain stopped and the sun came out – typical! No matter, through all of that, somehow, we had managed to qualify 7th, and given that people couldn't get a "second fastest" lap in, they used that result for the first two races, so we'd start 7th for races 1 and 2 that weekend.

Funnily enough, we hadn't learnt anything in that qualifying session, so had no further data to make any changes before the first race. The weather was playing havoc with our decision making, raining briefly, then stopping, revealing a hard beating sun and drying the track out, constantly going back and forth between the two. With time running thin before the start of the race, and no clear decisive call on the horizon, we made the gamble to go with a dry setup. The rain had eased and the sun was shining, but was it enough to dry the track?

Much like that of the first two meetings that year, Cadwell Park doesn't offer much in the way of allowing you to warm up brakes and tyres. You enter the track at the start of the third sector, just as you enter the woodland section. This does give you to twists and turns of the final section of track, but as you can't build much speed up, it's tricky to get the brakes warmed up to go with it.

Lights out! I was able to get a good start off the line, quickly latching onto the back of Matt Graux, before a number of the faster cars flew past. I was struggling to get the tyres and brakes switched on in the cool and damp conditions but as the corners ticked by, I could start to feel the car coming more alive. It wasn't long before our little gaggle around 10th place had formed a little convoy, led by Matt. We circled around like this for a lap or so, until the safety car was deployed for a stricken Danny Andrew just after the mountain. The safety car coming out gave me a good chance to try and get some proper heat into the tyres and brakes before the inevitable restart. The marshals did a fantastic job of recovering the car, as always, and it was only a lap before the green flag was out again.

Unfortunately, in the haste of people trying to get going, and a minor misjudgement from the leaders, there was a small pile-up heading into the final corner. It's common practice in motor racing for the leader (who controls the pace of the field before a restart) to back the pack up to try and make "the jump" on everyone by speeding away when they see fit. The one rule, however, is that when you go, you go! In my position buried somewhere in the mid-field, I cannot confirm exactly what happened here for sure, but I can confirm that exiting the penultimate corner, everyone ahead of me dove for the throttle and gunned it away, before standing on the brakes for the last corner and piling up into one gaggled mess. My assumption is whoever was leading had a change of heart, but no matter. Fortunately, there was no damage to anyone involved, more than the odd bit of rubber unceremoniously torn from their tyres from locking wheels, and after everyone had complied themselves again, the race got underway once more. I managed to tag onto the back of David Bowen, who was in turn chasing Matt Graux, with Dave Mason hot on my heels. Our little 4-car train chased up to the tight right hander at Park where David managed to slip past Matt. I tried my best to follow him through into the next corner, but this only allowed Dave Mason around the outside of me, who then in turn had his shot at trying around Matt into the next corner – we were very nearly going three wide into a corner that's tight enough going one wide! Unfortunately, Matt (in the middle of our little Ma7da sandwich) got a small kick of oversteer on the damp track and caught Dave, resulting in them both having to pull off the track and retire from the race – big shame for the two of them. This however, left me free to go hunting Mr Bowen with some clear track around me. Unfortunately, despite my best efforts, I was unable to catch him up, and still struggling with the setup in the tricky conditions, Tim Penstone-Smith and David Jones were both able to catch up and overtake me in the closing laps of the race. As we crossed the line to take the chequered flag, I was a little disappointed at our pace, but glad about another race finish, and we could hopefully now work on making some improvements to the setup for the races tomorrow. Upon returning back to the paddock, I was told that after everything the race had given, I'd still managed to finish in 10th place, which I was absolutely over the moon with – I really thought we were going to be massively further back than that. So, we went about making some changes to the car that evening before walking the track and trying to work out where all of this missing pace was!

Sunday morning came upon us and the sun shone through. No wind and no sign of clouds, so hopefully today would be better. We'd made changes to the car the previous night and we were hoping to be able to find some more pace, more toward what the car was performing like at Mallory. Our first race of the day wasn't until 11:05 in the morning, so we had the rare luxury of a nice lie-in.

Eventually, race time was upon us and we were called to the holding area. There had been a fair sprinkling of rain throughout the couple of races before ours, and although it had stopped and the sun was now shining, seeing how long it took the track to dry yesterday, we thought it would be the smart call to soften the car off and put a more wet-orientated setup on the car, to hopefully give it a bit more grip around the damper parts of the track. As it turns out, not for the first time this weekend, that call would in fact be the wrong one!

As we pulled onto the track and through the woodland section of the Cadwell Park circuit, I was feeling fairly confident in our call. However, as I pulled through the last corner and onto the start finish straight, seeing the ribbon of sun-dried tarmac before me, I did mumble "BOLLOCKS!" under my breath.

The lights went out, and once again we had a fairly acceptable start – or so I thought! As I pulled onto the Park Straight, I'd lost 3 positions, and was mere corners away from dropping a couple more. Turns out, what felt like a perfectly acceptable start from in the seat, was anything but. Come the end of the first lap however, the faster cars around me had made their moves, and I was now able to settle into the race. I wasn't feeling comfortable in the car still. The tyres we had on the car had done every racing lap so far this year and clearly needed changing. New car, new formula and new tyres, it's always a difficult one to judge how long these things last. No matter, head down, let's see what we can do!

It wasn't long before I was back on the bumper of Matt Graux, much like in the first race. Although the car wasn't feeling particularly good through the corners, I could tell that I had a bit more pace than him at this point in the race, and desperately wanted to capitalise on it. I will admit at this point, that I was quickly learning that I'm not the biggest fan of Cadwell Park. Although a fantastic track to drive, the layout and nature of the track doesn't lend itself to much in the way of overtaking opportunities, and means that you need to have a large pace advantage over your competitors to be able to make a move on them. Therefore, you spend most of your lap setting up a move, only for them to defend in the right point on the circuit, and all that setup you've been doing is now wasted because there is a car right where you need to be. All this was proven quite clearly to me in this race. Unfortunately, I had the pace advantage over Matt, but he was doing a brilliant job of defending at precisely the right points; meaning all the advantage I would setup over half the lap were negated when I really needed it. Nonetheless, we were having a spectacular tussle for the majority of the race, trying here, there and everywhere to make the move on him, but just never able to finish it off.

Eventually, after about ¾ of the race toiling away, I was able to sneak down the inside of him in Park and make the move stick. This move opened the door for the #3 car of Callum Barnes to follow me through. Callum and I then spent the rest of the race tussling it out between us for what would turn out to be 9th place, chopping and changing one after another, normally into the heavy braking zone of Park Corner. It was however on the final lap of the race that Callum made a small mistake coming through Chris Curve, selecting 2nd instead of 4th and putting himself on a mini, half spin. Overall, I was very pleased with the outcome of the race, as although still not completely happy with the car, we had at least made some improvement on the first race. As is customary in the Ma7da championships, all the drivers met up, shook hands and exchanged their respects for each other in Parc Ferme – without a doubt one of my favourite bits of this championship is the respect and comradery between the drivers and team members.

A couple of hours past, allowing the dust to settle from the second race of the weekend, before race 3 beckoned. The sun was beating down hard on us for the final race of the weekend. We had seen it all over the last couple of days, sun, torrential rain, lightning, thunder, but it was nice to end with some spectacular blue skies once again.

More confident with the conditions of this race, we went back to what we had ran in the first race, being a much stiffer, dry setup in the hopes that this would pay dividends. For the final time of the weekend, the lights went out, and for reasons unbeknownst to me, I got a terrible start – absolutely appalling, despite doing the same thing I had done all weekend. Watching the footage back, the engine looked to have almost stalled and re-started during the launch, akin to what you would see in the Formula 1 when their "anti-stall" kicks in. Regardless, due to the start, I dropped down a couple of places from my 9th place grid position before being able to settle into the race. It only took about the first lap or so before I was starting to feel confident in the car, and it wasn't long after that before I was starting to push on and challenge for positions. I was able to get a cracking run through the final corner and into turn one to make a move on David Jones, before carrying this momentum to get a good run down towards Park Corner and around the outside of Matt Graux. Unfortunately, I got a little too excited at this point and slightly outbraked myself into the next corner, allowed Matt back through. Undeterred by my little session of grass cutting, I was right back on him, hot on the heels to make it back through again. Much like we had in the previous races, I tried and tried different lines and attacks, but he did another brilliant job of defending against me. As we battled through the laps, Callum Barnes once again caught up to our little duel and started filling my mirrors as I tried to do so to Matt. A spectacular double move from Callum, not long after, saw him down the inside of me into Park, before diving across the grass to overtake Matt into the Gooseneck. I did my best to follow him, but was unable to do so. Only about half a lap later, I was able to sneak through around the outside of Matt through turn 2, and start trying to catch the runaway #3 car ahead.

Lap after lap I picked away at Callum, slowly

bringing the distance down until there were 2 laps to go - the battle was on!

At this point, I wasn't sure what position was on the cards, but I could taste another place to be had, and I wasn't going to give up until I had it. As we sped down towards Park once again, I could see Callum starting to weave across the track, clearly trying to break my tow. I firmly kept my wheels in his tracks and did what I could to keep my car as large in his mirrors as I could. Wrestling as we headed through the woodland section, I braked as late as I dared for the penultimate corner and closed right up behind him.

Final lap board shown.

Once again, we head down towards Park Corner almost as one, and I poke my nose around the outside of him but he was able to hold it on the inside through the corner. We follow, nose to tail through Chris Curve, the Gooseneck and into Mansfield and at this point I was starting to think this might not be doable, there are only so many opportunities around this track. We speed towards the chicane at the Mountain and he got a slight twitch of oversteer and I saw my opportunity. Planting my foot on the loud pedal, I got a big kick of oversteer myself and rode the four-wheel-drift through the exit of the chicane and up the Mountain, sliding alongside him as we joined the stretch into the woodland section. I was on the inside and braked as late as I dared, sliding just in front, but losing the rear slightly through the right and left kinks. Able to hold it, we were quickly on the anchors for the penultimate corner once again. He stuck his nose down the inside for a look into the final corner, but was unable to make the move stick as we pulled onto the final straight to take the chequered flag. #79 claiming another 10th place.

What a race that had been! Absolutely epic from flag to flag – this is what it's all about. As we pulled into Parc Ferme for the final time that weekend, Callum and his dad were the first to congratulate me, and I them, for what he been a true spectacle of racing from both sides. By the time Mum, Dad and Bex had made it over from their viewing platform on the other side of the track, I'd shaken hands with most of the team members of the grid who were watching from the café, and got a firsthand view of my move into the Hail Bends. As luck would have it, Dad apparently was looking elsewhere when I had made the move, and was profusely shouted at by Bex and my Mum for not paying attention. Apparently the final few seconds of the race waiting for me to emerge in front of or behind Callum as I was lost from view, were some of the tensest of Bex's life, and who could blame her! My heartrate wasn't exactly slow at that point either!

How can I sum up the weekend here at Cadwell Park? Beats me, as I write this now, I've had a whole month to think it over and try and come up with a suitable summary, and I still can't think of the right words. Was I happy with the performance? Absolutely, how could I not be! Was I a little frustrated at struggling with the setup of the car for so long? Once again, absolutely, how could I not be! That is the beautiful, and painful thing about racing. You are always going to have your good days and bad days; unfortunately, even with an unlimited supply of money, that will always happen! I don't think I could even dream of labelling our weekend at Cadwell as a bad one – three top 10 finishes! How could you label that as bad? Bex asked me on the way up on Friday, "What would you be happy with this weekend?" and my response was 3 top 10 finishes. To achieve that I thought was amazing, as I really thought that those top 10s were unlikely. I think coming into this meeting after the success of Mallory was the biggest struggle here, but a track this complicated is never something you will be able to get the hang of quickly. I will however stand by my earlier comment about not particularly liking the place. Cannot fault it as a drivers track, and if you have never been there, I highly recommend you give it a try, because it challenges so much of a driver, and is really something when you get it all right. However, as a racing track, I just can't like it. There are a very limited number of overtaking opportunities around the track, unless you have a big pace advance over your competitor. Compare it to somewhere like Anglesey, which is probably comparably long, but you can overtake on almost every corner. Therefore, will I be upset if it's missing from the calendar next year? Absolutely not, I might even have a beer to celebrate! Will I be upset if it is featured? Meh, probably not – I feel I need to come back with some more experience and have another go, I'm far too stubborn to let a track beat me like this!

CHAPTER 18 – HAPPY BIRTHDAY MUM!

Date: 11/07/2023

Time: 17:00

Location: The Garage

Today is Mum's 50th birthday. Young Mr Dave gave her a shoutout at the trophy presentation on the weekend (which I promise we didn't ask for!), and Bex and I carpet bombed the awning and van with birthday banners in anticipation of their arrival on Saturday. Hey, they could definitely tell which one was ours couldn't they! Following the weekend of excitement, the two of them have headed off to France for a couple of weeks for a nice getaway in the motorhome. Bon Voyage!

Right, onto more race-car-y things! The lead up to the meeting at Cadwell Park had ended up being a rather hectic affair. Through no direct fault of my own, there were a couple of bits that we were waiting to get delivered, or waiting to get fitted to the car, and this had been the case for most of the meetings this year – I intended to change that from here-on out! After taking the Monday off following the weekend, I was down the garage straight from work on Tuesday to put together the list of jobs that needed doing on the car before the next meeting out at Brands Hatch. I am a big fan of Brands, and have raced there a couple of times before, so this could be my best opportunity for a high scoring result all season. We also made the call to take the car there testing before the meeting, to try and work on dialling-in the setup, and also to give me a chance to learn how the different setups affect the car directly. Before we got to any of that however, we had to get through this list first.

- Passenger Seat Modifications
- Handbrake
- Sort Bias Adjuster
- Full Service
- Other Misc Tasks

Clearly, not the worst of lists to work through, but by no means the best. The car had been very reliable at Cadwell, with no real work needed mechanically. However, we had nearly 7 weeks before the next meeting out, and the car had been raced hard for half a season now with only regular maintenance tasks undertaken on it. Therefore, I decided to go all out.

Going back to late 2022 when this whole idea was nothing more than a pipedream, I wanted to fit a passenger seat in my car so we'd have the opportunity to take friends, family and potential sponsors out on the track to give them a feel for what it's like. This was one of the longest gaps we'd get between meetings all year, so I thought "why not?". It wasn't long before the car, working perfectly that previous weekend, was torn apart and spewed across the side of the workshop, revealing the chassis so I could weld on my new brackets.

Along with the modifications to suit the passenger seat in the car, I also worked on a new handbrake design. Up until now, we had been running a hydraulic handbrake, similar to those used in rally and drift cars – the "giggle stick" as I referred to it. However, it was a big and bulky solution, and required the re-bleeding of the brakes every time it was fitted or removed, should we fit a passenger seat in. I wanted a much neater solution that can be kept as is regardless of the extra seat being installed or not. Unfortunately, I had run out of time to install my new bits before Cadwell, as the parts turned up on the Monday AFTER the meeting!

Next on the list was the bias adjuster. Done in the dying seconds before getting the car out for testing at the start of the season, the bias adjuster (which, if you don't know already, is a small dial mounted in the car that allows you to adjust the brake pressure forwards and backwards in the car. Locking the front wheels too easily, dial it back – locking the rear wheels too easily, dial it forwards) was mounted in a "less than ideal" position, being just out of my reach when fully belted in – I could adjust it, but it required being on a straight, off throttle, and leaning as far as I possibly could while still strapped in. Clearly, not the ideal solution to adjust in the heat of battle when out on the track. Cue a new bias adjuster being bought, and a new bracket fitted to the chassis to suit, and now the dial comes easily to the hand for adjustment on the move – ideal!

And finally, (although not one task, but a series of small bits and bobs) the full service. The poor little #79 car had been very well looked after at this point in the season. We bolt check it after every session and give it a thorough check over after every meeting. We check the oil levels and water levels frequently, and it's washed and polished before every meeting. The biggest thing with motorsport is it's all in the preparation work. You can be the fastest driver on the track, but if the car isn't maintained well and breaks down on you, being the fastest out there is rather a moot point. Therefore, I opted to give the car a thorough service before the next meeting. Pulling out and changing the oils where needed, checking brake pads, checking callipers – things like that. Although it may not guarantee you any better reliability or higher performance, it does give you peace of mind. As it turns out in this instance, the brake pads had in fact glazed over. We aren't sure if this happened at Cadwell, or if it was done at Mallory, but if it was in fact done at Mallory, it would give a bit of reason as to why the brakes weren't quite up to scratch around Cadwell. Proof that checking the car over after every meeting could save you the odd bit of time here and there if you find something you are missing!

CHAPTER 19 – TIME TO GET BACK TO BUSINESS.

Date: 16/08/2023

Time: 09:00

Location: Brands Hatch

The week leading up to the next meeting at Brands Hatch saw the rarely seen Test Day in the Team Rogers camp. Typically, between work and budget restrictions, we are unable to go away and get testing in, but for the upcoming meeting, we felt we had to make the exception. Brands is a track I have loved for a long time, despite having a terrible track record there (pun certainly not intended). As well as this, since building the car, we haven't been able to explore the different alterations we can make on the setup fully, so the day at Brands today should give us ample opportunity to get a feel for what the different changes will do to the handling. Dad and I made the journey up in the van, and a friend of mine, Tom, has also come to offer a hand spannering for me.

Drivers briefing completed, noise testing done and now with the sighting laps completed, we were ready to hit the track. Dad and I had been over a bit of a game plan for the day, with me explaining everything I wanted to get from the day of running, and us agreeing that whatever changes he wanted to try, I was more than happy to go along with. I think the description from him was "I'll make the changes, and you be the dumb driver behind the wheel and tell me if the changes were good or bad" – call it what you want, the system worked! We went out for countless runs of about 5 laps a piece, having a go with all sorts of different combinations of setup, eventually working towards the "perfect" setup on the car. I've no doubt the setup is by no means "perfect", but it was a good starting point for us to try the following weekend, and it gave me a good chance to get a feel for what every change was doing to the feel of the car beneath me.

The thing that shocked me the most about our day out in the sun, was how fast this thing was compared to the other exotics at the trackday. We had opted to go for the cheaper option of a standard track day, meaning you are free to go out as much or as little as you want, but you are mixed in with anything and everything all at once. No "racing" is allowed, and if you have a faster car behind you, you need to let them through. But our little 1800 Locost on its road legal tyres was taking on and beating most things – Porsches, BMWs, Can-Am Cars, you name it, they all had to let us through! I think there were only a couple of cars throughout the whole day that we consistently had to let through, but they were a Radical, and a Westfield with a screaming motorbike engine and wings bigger than the car – I think they deserved to be faster!

Overall, we had an absolutely cracking day. There were a couple of our Ma7da friends there for the day too, soaking up the rays and getting some track time in preparation for the upcoming meeting. We were absolutely stunned with the improvements we had made to the car, and I was buzzing for the meeting here in 10 days' time. Fingers crossed we can utilise our newfound pace and try and fight our way up the grid that bit further.

CHAPTER 20 – 400 MILES, 18 HOURS AND 2 RACES

Date: 26/08/2023

Time: 04:30

Location: Brands Hatch

My alarm was set for 3:30am and I could not sleep – I was super excited for the 5th meeting of the year, this time at Brands Hatch. It had been the best part

ONE TYRE FIRE

of 6 weeks since we were out at Cadwell Park and I was ready for the next couple of races. The van was loaded and we hit the road at just before 5 in the morning. People always question us why we don't travel up on a Friday night so we don't have to do a stupid-O-clock start in the morning to get to the meeting, but if you have ever tried to get to Brands Hatch on a Friday night in rush hour traffic on the M25, you'll probably understand.

We got to the track bright and early, and since the day here testing last week, any and all changes and checks had been made to the car in preparation – all we needed to do was torque the wheels and set the tyre pressures. This single day event was lining itself up to be a really good day; on one of my favourite tracks in the world, we had various family and friends joining us to support me, and the weather was supposed to be good for both of our races – couldn't ask any more than that! In fact, the only thing missing was Bex as she was away at the football for the day so couldn't join us.

We were all setup in the paddock, we'd had a wonder round a said hello to everyone and it wasn't long before we were called for qualifying. I've never done particularly well in qualifying as a general rule of thumb, but I always enjoy it. Doing everything you can to try and squeeze every drop of juice out of your lap time, getting a feel for the days running and finding the limits of the track and the car – amazing. I was queued first to leave the holding area this morning, quite a rare occurrence that is! Slowly but surely however, all of the drivers started filling in behind me, including one 1300 Ford Locost which I assumed was only there to get his three laps in, because I think he'd probably struggle putting in a lap to compete with us!

It wasn't long after that when the whistle was blown and we headed out through the pit lane and onto the track. The hardest part about leading the field onto the track is you are the first one to dip your toe into the conditions. Fortunately for me, the track was bone dry and the sun was shining, so conditions were perfect. As we left the track when we were here testing a week and a half ago, the car was absolutely on rails and I loved how it was driving. I was hoping that as nothing had changed on the car, this would more than likely be the case, but as it turned out, not for the first time this season, I was wrong!

Dad informed me after the session that Brands is very well known for its changeable track condition. You think you get the car running absolutely perfect one weekend, and then the next weekend in what you think are the same conditions, the car feels completely different. Clearly, what had worked for us a week ago was no longer doing it. Out on the track I was fighting oversteer and understeer at any and all points in every corner. There is nothing you can adjust in the car other than brake bias, so I was very much left to sort it out on my own. It didn't seem to matter how hard I pushed or how gently I worked the pedals or the steering, the car just wasn't responding well. I even tried tucking in behind a couple of the quicker cars to try and learn what they were doing, and despite braking in a similar place and taking a line identical to theirs, the car just wouldn't do what theirs would. I was getting more and more frustrated in the car and was over the moon when the chequered flag came out. This was the first time I had explicitly disliked a session on track in this car, and when I got back to the paddock and was told that the best I had done was 15th - you can imagine my mood!

We spent the next half hour going through the lap, piece by piece, and what the car was doing throughout, before eventually deciding on the changes we wanted to make before the first race. Although I wasn't best pleased with the result, Dad was happy that although we were a little further off than we had hoped, and 1.5 seconds off the pace of the leaders, I had come back complaining that the car was terrible to drive. If we'd come off the track saying the car was perfect and we were 1.5 seconds off, then that would be a problem, but at least this way, we knew there was time to be made up.

When you are starting down in 15th out of 20 cars,

making a couple of drastic changes to the setup on the car doesn't feel too bad as hopefully you can find the missing piece of the puzzle and start moving forwards. If you get it wrong however, you aren't losing out on too much. As it turned out, the setup changes weren't too far off.

We were called for the first race and as I sat in the holding area, I was quietly confident. Although not happy with the performance in qualifying, I was hopeful that the changes we had made will start to drag us that bit further up. Plus, I do love overtaking people, so if we had made the car better, it should mean that we've got an exciting race lined up!

In the hour leading up to the first race, the heavens had opened something chronic, and the track was soaked. Our little team were huddled together under the awning for shelter, but eventually it passed and a hot sunshine broke through. This, over the course of about 15 minutes had managed to almost completely dry the circuit out, giving us the dry race we had all hoped for. However, because of the damp patches on the track, the officials had given us a single green flag lap to get our eye in for the conditions on the circuit. Personally, I don't agree with the whole "No Green Flag Lap" thing with our formula as it seems very dangerous to me. You head into the first corner not really knowing how much grip you have beneath you, and with brake pads that haven't had a chance

ONE TYRE FIRE

to warm up yet – I think it's silly! That being said, I guess it's an argument to be made about the talent of a driver. If you can get in and give it everything straight away, regardless of the car beneath you, then I doff my cap to you, fair play! However, the blessing of one warm up lap for this race was gratefully received! Eventually, tyres and brakes warmed, we pulled up to the line. I was perched on the right-hand side of the track on a slight downhill section, and was struggling to balance the brakes, throttle and clutch as the lights were waiting to go out. It felt like an eternity, but eventually they were extinguished and the race was underway!

Straight off the mark, I didn't have the best of starts, lighting the tyres up in first and second which quickly allowed Ian Wells past me on the inside and as we ran up to Paddock Hill Bend for the first time, I was completely boxed in, from all angles. If someone were to lose it right now, there would be a completely unavoidable 5-car pileup for sure! Fortunately, as I was now accustomed to in this formula, all the drivers involved were very courteous and professional in their driving, and our little cluster stormed into Druids Hairpin. Still locked in place, it felt like we were about 20-cars wide through the corner, when it reality it was probably about 2 or 3. However, as we exited the corner, we all started to file into line and I was finally able to start getting my head down and making some moves. My old sparring partner from Anglesey, Imran Khan, was back in the seat of the #21 car this weekend and he was now lined right in front of me as we headed through Graham Hill Bend. I tried my luck down the inside of him out of Clearways, but got caught as he went around the outside of Stephen Kimber. I tried to follow suit, but was unable to make the move as we headed into Paddock for the second time. An excellent run through the corner from myself, and as we headed into Druids, I sent it around the outside of Kimber and hung it all the way to cinch the place as we headed into Graham Hill once more. A poor exit from me however allowed him to snatch it right back, and as we crossed the start line, the positions remained as they had the lap previous. Seeing how well the move into Druids had worked the last lap, I was spurred on to try it again this time, but maybe without the cock-up through Graham Hill to ruin it again! I licked the stamp and sent it, and this time I had the move complete before the next corner, so could take the proper racing line and maintain the position. The next couple of laps were then spent tussling positions with Imran and rookie this weekend, Robert Guymer. Eventually, I managed to take what was then 15th position from Imran over the course of nearly half a lap side by side, starting off in Paddock Hill Bend, and not completing the move until we headed into Surtees.

Finally, 5 laps into the race, and I had managed to make my way back to where I had started it. I was now about 5 car lengths behind Matt Graux, another sparring partner of mine from earlier in the season, and Ian Wells who did a fantastic job of leapfrogging me at the start. Imran was breathing down my neck behind, so all I could do was try to push on to the next car. The laps tumbled by and eventually I managed to catch the back of the #34 car of Graux, with a couple of car lengths clear between myself and Khan. Matt had proven himself to be a wizard at keeping cars behind him at Cadwell, and I had no doubt he would be pretty handy here too, so I was hoping for a quick and clean move past him, but unfortunately that was not the case. At this point, we were about halfway through the race and I spent pretty much every last racing lap doing what I could to get past him, but it was to no avail. With about 4 minutes left of the race, Anthony Ridd and David Winter had a coming together and ended up parked in the gravel at Paddock Hill Bend. So close to the end of the race, I was certain we were going to end under caution. And as expected, about 3 laps behind the safety car later, the chequered flag was flown. A shame to end under safety car, but no matter, we had had a cracking race, and with the two cars dropping out, we had finished in 13th place. Maybe not as high up as I was hoping, but still struggling with the performance of the car, I would take that.

One of the biggest things that I had noticed from race 1, and it must have been fairly noticeable, because everyone in the team watching from the sidelines had also commented on it, was that we were clearly lacking some straight-line performance over our competitors. Regardless of how well I would get out of a corner, come the end of the next straight they would have pulled a number of lengths on me. In a championship as tightly controlled as this, something like that just isn't possible, so there must be something wrong with our car. The only thing we could think of causing this problem was the cam timing as there isn't much else that can alter during the course of a race. There is a cover over the front of the engine, so in theory this getting changed shouldn't be possible, but we thought it was worth a try nonetheless! Therefore, we opted not to touch the setup on the car, and instead pull the front of the engine off and check the timing. Amazingly, we had found that it had jumped a tooth on the inlet cam – this would certainly cause a slight lack in power. We therefore fixed the timing problem, put the front end back together and prepped the car for the final race of the day. How long we had this timing issue will be another one of those things we will never know. We hadn't checked the cam timing of the engine all year, since building it way back early in January. We'd have set it right then, but as the belt wears over time, it stretches, and it's assumed that this is what had caused the tooth to jump. It's possible it happened at Croft and that's what caused the rough running in that first race. It could have happened on the last lap of testing a week and a half prior to this meeting. It will remain one of those mysteries.

The weather stayed on our side for the remainder of our time here at Brands, so as we were called for the final race, although a little cloudy in places, the conditions were pretty good! At this point, we had no idea what to expect for the final race. Was the timing change going to make any difference? If it made any difference, was it going to be noticeable? If it was noticeable, would the setup handle the difference in power or would it be too lively on the rear? The list went on, but these things were playing in my mind. I was hopeful that we had found something.

As the conditions were fine for this race, we were back to usual programming with no Green Flag Lap. This means the short run to the line is packed full of desperately trying to get everything switched on in the car before dutifully taking your place on the grid. I was starting in 15th again this race, which although annoying, did give me an idea of what I was heading into. I knew the road dropped slightly downhill, I knew it was in the middle, and I knew there was room for a car to slip through on my right. As it turned out, the change to the timing of the engine made a massive difference to the power and torque it was producing, and this caught me out massively as the red lights were extinguished and the race got underway. Far too much wheelspin off the line meant that Stephen Kimber was right down my inside as we headed for the first corner, but seeing a gap appearing, and knowing how much grip there was around the outside of Druids in the first race, I opted to take the slightly unconventional line, and move to the outside of the track. With everyone defending against each other into and through Druids, my plan worked perfectly, and I was able to slip around the outside of Matt Graux and line up Ian Wells for an overtake later in the lap too. The next car on my hit list was Robert Guymer. The two of us battled hard for the proceeding lap, before I had a nibble down the inside into Paddock, and he unfortunately lost the back end and slid into the gravel trap, bringing out the yellow flags in sector 1 so they could do a live snatch of the car to safety. I was hoping they would send the safety car out, but such was not the case. A lap or so later, I was hot on the heels of Stephen Kimber, who I had had some fantastic battles with that weekend, and with the yellows at Paddock, I managed to once again send it around the outside through Druids Hairpin. After this, I was left on my own for a fair few laps chasing the cars in front. That was until Callum Barnes had a moment going through Graham Hill Bend and rejoined the track right in front of me – thus re-igniting the flame of our battle at Cadwell Park.

It was a little before the halfway point of the race – game on. Unfortunately, the yellow flags were still being waved halfway down the start finish straight, which eliminated one of the better overtaking opportunities on the circuit, so the green flag wasn't being shown until heading into turn 2, Druids. This therefore meant that the two of us were simply following line-astern for a few laps while I tried to work out the best place to mount my attack. We crossed the halfway point of the race and joy of joys, the yellow flags were no longer being flown down the start finish straight, so it was on. On the first fully green lap, I had a nose to the outside of Paddock, which gave me a terrific opportunity to cut back and go for it down the inside of Druids. I managed to pull alongside the #3 car, but a big kick of oversteer at the apex of the corner let Callum get the legs on me down towards Graham Hill. Notice of intent had now been formally served. The next lap, I tried the exact same move again, but this time was unable to sneak down the inside at Druids and had to reside the next lap to starting at the rear bumper of the car in front. Another good run out of clearways and onto the start finish straight and this time I was able to make a much more convincing move into Druids. The two cars alongside one another into, through and out of the corner all the way down towards Graham Hill. I opted to try something a little different here, and sold Callum a dummy down the outside, before cutting back to the inside, hoping he would outbrake himself and I could sneak through. By some miracle, the move worked and I took the position from him and tried to break away from him. Unfortunately for me, but this point in the race, having battled hard with Callum for a number of laps by now, and already struggling with the setup of the car with the additional ponies now residing under the bonnet, I was unable to make the break and Callum made it back past me a few corners later after I had another big oversteer moment at Paddock, Druids and Graham Hill the following lap. Annoyingly, from there-on in, my fate was sealed. With rear tyres overheating it was a battle to try and keep the car under control for the rest of the race, and I had to concede defeat and eventually take the chequered flag in 10th place. This result was improved however when Danny Andrew was given a time penalty for overtaking under yellow flags, and I was moved up to 9th.

Overall, although not as successful as we were hoping, we thoroughly enjoyed our time at Brands Hatch and are looking forward to hopefully coming back next year – hopefully with a better setup on the car though!

CHAPTER 21 – SO, WHAT WAS GOING WRONG?

Date: 28/08/2023

Time: 17:00

Location: The Garage (thinking caps donned)

The one-day event of Brands Hatch has now been and gone. Although we had a lovely time away, enjoyed seeing everyone and had some cracking racing throughout, there was one rather large elephant lurking in the garage (figuratively of course, you couldn't fit an elephant in the garage!). All season long we had been getting better and better with every meeting, making big improvements in the car, and then in myself at the track. Cadwell Park was always going to be one of the worst meetings of the year in my head as it's a very long and complex track that I'd never driven before, and on the contrary, I always had in my head that Brands Hatch was going to be one of my best. Sat here percolating on the events of the past weekend, the reality was very much a polar opposite. Although Cadwell was by no means one of the best meetings of the year from my viewpoint, the results were undeniably the best we had gotten all year, scoring 3 top 10 finishes. Brands Hatch, with the struggles of the setup, turned out to be the worst of the season (if you don't include the first meeting at Croft, being the first time out in the car). So, what had gone wrong? After the day testing at Brands, I was fairly confident that we had finally hit the nail on the head. I was pretty sure that we had tackled the bulk of the big-ticket setup changes and now had a car that would just need a little bit of fettling to suit the track on a meeting-by-meeting basis, however the results very much disagreed with that.

So, what had been going wrong? Once I'd captured all of the footage of the meeting, I went through it piece-by-piece and tried to work out where our biggest issues were, and could find two almost straight away. Fortunately, a number of other drivers also upload their footage onto YouTube, so I was able to watch what they were doing and how their cars were behaving compared to mine. Almost instantly I could tell that my car was incredibly nervous heading into corners. Watching the other drivers, their cars were almost completely planted to the track every time they turned into a corner; whereas, on nearly every corner, I was having to put in a small correction before I even made it to the apex. Adding to that, my car was understeering something chaotic compared to the others, and this was forcing me to take the corners considerably slower than everyone else just to keep the car on the track.

At the testing day, we played around with the mounting points for the trailing arms. On our cars, we are allowed to have 3 different mounting points where the trailing arms (which are the links joining the rear axle to the chassis) can mount to. Our cars have to run a 4-link setup, using 2 trailing arms on either side of the axle, all mandated at the same length. All this means, that these mounting points give a variety of handling characteristics depending on where you bolt the arms in. Use the middle holes and the axle doesn't do anything funny, and you'll have fairly neutral handling. The top and bottom holes allow the axle to rotate as you roll through the corner and load the outside wheel. Use to the top hole and the axle rotates away from the corner, creating rear wheel steer and therefore a tighter turning radius, but also inducing oversteer. Use the bottom hole and it does the opposite, steering the axle towards the corner and therefore preventing the car from oversteering, and therefore inducing understeer. After the day testing at Brands, knowing the car rather enjoys oversteering and catching me out at the worst times, we had opted to run the car with the links on the bottom, making the car understeer, but preventing it from oversteering. On the baking hot day testing, this worked an absolute treat, and I could really throw the car into the corners and it would stick like nothing I had driven all year! However, this setup on a colder, damp day just didn't work. All this did in fact was make the car understeer massively through the corners. So fortunately, we were able to quickly deduce where the massive understeer was coming from, but that was only half of the issues – why was it so nervous on the rear end going into the corners?

As I write this today, I will admit that we still don't have the answer. I have spent many evenings watching footage back from the year and reading books, researching online, and practicing on the computer, trying different setup techniques to try and work out what I think the problem is. We have a number of theories what could be causing it, but until we get the car out again, we just aren't going to know what it is. So, for now, I will have to word it as "blind optimism!". If we are in fact correct with our best guesses heading into the final meeting of the year, and the car is on rails, then hallelujah! If, however, the car still isn't working correctly then it will be a long winter trying to work out what is causing that, no pressure eh!

So, with our fault finding for Silverstone all but

complete, and the fate of our pace primarily in the hands of the racing gods, the mood now turns to what can we do to make the car faster? If we assume for now that our setup changes are in fact correct and the car is no longer going to handle like a blind pig in a thunderstorm, then we want to see what else we can do to the car to try and eek that final little bit of speed out of it. Silverstone GP is a very big circuit, and one I have only driven once before in the real world. I am not the biggest fan of it personally, as it is just too big for "normal" cars. Take your 1000 horsepower screaming Le Mans Prototype there and I'm sure it feels fine, but in a 150-horsepower shoebox, it's a very long lap. My guess is there are going to be at least 10-15 seconds sat flat out just going down each of the long straights. I know people think that the big, fast tracks are the most interesting to drive, but I just find them dull; give me a Mallory, Lydden Hill or Knockhill over Silverstone, Snetterton or Donington any day!

Anyway, back on track! What can we do to make the car just that little bit faster? As I have covered numerous times in this book, there isn't much scope to make these cars faster than they already are. If you are struggling to grasp what these cars look like, find an empty shoebox (a filled shoebox will also do) and look at it from across the room while squinting your eyes. I can assure you that that shoebox looks a lot like a Mazda-seven right about now! So, what I'm getting at, is that within the regulations, there isn't really anything you can do to make these cars streamlined. That doesn't mean that there aren't gains to be made however, quite the opposite. Because the cars aerodynamics are so bad, all the little bits do make a difference, and on a track like Silverstone, these little differences will more than likely add up to some considerable lap time. So, although I had read the championship regulations about 20 times by this point in the season, I took it upon myself as a race engineer to re-read them again, this time looking for the slightly more obscure, darker corners of the regs. Unfortunately, as they have been written very well, there aren't many loopholes to find without blatantly breaking the rules. However, that doesn't mean that I was unable to find some areas.

Up until this point in the season, I have been running a "floor-less" car – that being a car with no floor, there are plenty of flaws in it, the driver undoubtedly being the biggest one! In the haste of building the car at the start of the year, I wasn't worried about things like floor panels (this is floor panels under the engine by the way, the cockpit and boot are mandated to have a floor), as the car would work fine without them. I did make me wonder though, how much faster the car might be with one fitted. The same point went for the sump guard, we are allowed to fit one within a tight limit of regulations. Maybe that will make a difference to the performance of the car? As well as these changes, a number of drivers run a "shield" behind the radiator which forces the hot air out the side of the car so it doesn't get trapped under the bonnet. And finally, we are allowed to run a "half-door" on the side of the car next to the driver, to reduce the wind catching on the driver, and hopefully make it more streamlined through the air.

Therefore, I had my shopping list and the task list was re-filled with things to be getting on with to (hopefully at least) make the car that bit better for Silverstone! Only time will tell if these changes were actually worthwhile, just 5 weeks to go until the finale to the 2023 season.

CHAPTER 22 – 3-CHEERS FOR EARLY STARTS! HIP-HIP...

Date: 12/10/2023

Time: 03:00 (am, just in case you were wondering!)

Location: My house

I should probably read back through this book and

count the times I've mentioned about early starts! Hopefully, you aren't bored of them, because here's another one for you.

Why oh why have I set a 3am alarm – must mean it's time to go racing again! Nope, don't worry, we aren't gunning for the best spot in the paddock to rock up 2 weeks early, we've made the call to have one last crack of testing before the final meeting of the year. Weighing up the options of trackdays between the car being finished about two weeks ago, and the final meeting in two weeks' time, we've decided to make the journey back to Mallory Park. Having gotten on there very well early in the year, we thought it would be a good stomping ground to get some more seat time in the car, and try out the setup changes that were made. Therefore, the alarm went off at 3, and we were wheels up, Mallory-bound by 430.

Much like at Brands earlier in the year, we'd opted for a "cheaper" all access trackday here today, on the gamble that everyone would play ball and be courteous, and no silly accidents were to be had (and just so no one worries, none were had! Mum, Nan, I'm looking in your corners ☐). The big difference with our trackday today, other than all the changes made to the car, was that for the first time ever, the #79 car was being piloted by someone other than myself. It may have taken almost the whole season, but I have managed to convince Dad to have a go in the car.

We arrived at the track bright and early, weary from fighting through the poor sods commuting to work, early on the Thursday morning. It had been raining all morning, but fortunately had ceased a few hours before we got there, so the track was damp but drying quickly. After signing on and noise test, we were off for our sighting laps.

The day very productive trying out a number of different settings on the car, figuring out what worked and what didn't, as well as getting some cracking seat time for me. Once the car was deemed "perfect" once again, we swapped drivers for Dad's first hot laps in the car, and he immediately shone to it. Having never driven a car like this, where you are exposed to the elements, I wasn't quite sure what he was going to make of it; but when he pulled back into the pits, and I could almost see his grin through the helmet. I recall him uttering the words "you've built one hell of a race car here" as he climbed out of the car.

As the day carried on, we continued trying a variety of different settings on the car, trying to work out any and all details that we could about the handling. We had managed to dial out all of the nervousness in the handling, and it was now absolutely glued to the track on corner entry. Where the car would start understeering out through the mid and exit parts of the corner at Brands, it was now tucking itself to the apex of the corner, with the gentle balancing of the throttle

ONE TYRE FIRE

keeping it from twitching the rear and sliding the front. It was handling like an absolute weapon! Between every meeting this year we have made a variety of changes to the car, and every time I have gotten back in the driver's seat and said, "this is the best the car has ever handled", but this time it was just something else. Up until now, I hadn't felt this comfortable in the car. Even the last time we were here at Mallory, where the car was the fastest it had been all year, this setup felt worlds better. Just to re-enforce if the setup was in fact better or not, I flicked the camera on for the final couple of runs I had throughout the day. The first of which, we were fairly happy with, and I was putting in some very good laps. The second run, we decided to try out a different setting on the front anti-rollbar. After about 15 minutes of running around, I got a good feel for the car, but was fairly confident that it was in fact slower. Dad (naughtily) tried to time a couple of the laps in this run to get a grasp for what it was doing lap time wise. We came in and reverted the changes back and I headed onto the track for the final time. Final run, and I was adamant that the car was faster with these settings. I recall even betting the ice creams on it that those laps were faster. Upon return to the pits, Dad read out the fastest laps, and it turned out I was in fact right, and about half a second quicker with the settings in the final run.

Upon return back home, I watched the camera

footage back with a timer to confirm that Dads timings were in fact correct, and our final run was the best part of half a second quicker on average than that of the previous. Notably alongside that, my fastest lap of the day was a 52.7 second lap, only 0.1 seconds off the fastest I had done earlier in the year. Given the lack of track temperature on the test day, and not having another car to chase, I was absolutely over the moon with that! Plus, although the 52.7 was our fastest lap, almost every other run in that "session" was a 52.8, only a tenth off that fastest lap. That proved that not only was the car faster, but it was consistent too! All of this was driving home far too much confidence heading into the final meeting of the year!

Silverstone is now 17 days away, and I cannot wait! If the car drives as well as it has today, this is going to be a fantastic finale to what has been a brilliant year's racing. Only time will tell now.

CHAPTER 23 – THE FINAL CHAPTER (FIGURATIVELY, THERE ARE MORE CHAPTERS

AFTER THIS ONE)

Date: 29/10/2023

Time: 08:00

Location: Silverstone Circuit

It's been a hell of a year! Back on New Years Day, we had no car, best part of no parts for the car we didn't have, and absolutely no clue what the year was going to bring. Fast forward to now, we've finished every race so far this year, have managed a number of top 10 finishes and an all-time best finish of 6th, have met some amazing people, and had countless laughs along the way. It's been an unforgettable season, one I will cherish for many years to come, but 2023 is not over yet. Heading into this meeting, by some miracle, the #79 car is ranked in 6th place overall. Martin West and David Mason are hot on my heels, only 4 and 6 points behind, respectively. Unfortunately for them, their lack of reliability for a couple of races have meant I've managed to squeeze in front. Annoyingly for me however, due to this championship running "drop scores" (meaning at the end of the year, you lose your two worst results), I will need an almighty miracle to maintain this 6th place as where things currently stand I will be losing 29 points, whereas they will only lose 2. Nonetheless,

8th place would be the worst I can finish without a catastrophic result this weekend, and if you don't count 2021 Locost Champion, Martin West, as a rookie, then I would be the highest scoring rookie of '23, so that in itself is a hell of a feat if you ask me!

We got to the track at a fairly reasonable 5pm last night, but this weekend is the Birkett Relay Race, a 6-hour endurance race held by the 750 Club which allows nearly any and all cars in a relay style endurance race. By this I mean that instead of teams sharing a car that has to last the full 6 hours, each driver has their own car, and they do stints before pulling into the pits, allowing the next car in the team to head onto the track. It's a race that has interested me for a number of years, and I would definitely be keen to give it a go, but given that this year we are racing the day after the event, have a serious problem in the relay race, and you are all but screwed for our races the following day! Maybe next year. However, because of the Birkett going on yesterday, the paddock was absolute carnage last night, so Dad and I just landed wherever we could find some space. As it turned out however, we managed quite a good spot with a host of our Ma7da friends around us.

This weekend, things are being run slightly differently than normal. Given the size of the circuit here at Silverstone, the decision was made by the higher powers that be, to have two races run simultaneously in each session this weekend, meaning that every formula is on track at the same time as another formula, and in our case, we are on with the Sports Specials. Sports Specials are a series of kit-car-esque vehicles, the full extent of the regulations, I'm not entirely sure about, but there was a hell of a mixture of stuff out there with us which really made it tricky gauging what you could follow and what you really couldn't!

As mentioned, Dad and I got to the track last night as our race meeting was all on the Sunday, meaning we had Saturday to travel up at a leisurely pace. Mum, Bex and a friend of ours, Allan, had all travelled up last night after Exeter's football and rugby games, and stayed in a hotel just down the road, and also Tom has also made the journey up to help this weekend too. Full house then, no pressure! Following our day testing at Mallory, I was super confident with the car, and hoping for a day of dry weather to give our new setup a real run for its money; however, as we were called for qualifying, the track was still very damp from the rain that had fallen the night before. The sun was out however, so we were hoping that the track was going to come to us soon enough, and we could really stretch our legs with the new settings.

Qualifying beckoned and it wasn't long before I was sat in the queue waiting to get noise tested and into the holding area. As I found my place in the queue, David Bowen (one of my new friends in the championship) pulled up behind me and was graciously trying his best to take the piss vicariously through his wife, Sam, who was running between mine and his cars passing messages like little schoolgirls. He also mentioned to me after the meeting that he spent the time having a nosey at my car and learning what he could about what we'd done – not sure what he was trying to learn though, he'd proven he was faster than me at nearly every meeting this year!

As the whistle blew and we headed out onto the track, I very quickly realised that we had definitely made the wrong call on the setup – I'm sensing a distinct theme with this this year! At Silverstone you can't see a massive amount of the track when you are in the paddock. You can have a little wander to different places, but getting a grasp on what it's like as a whole is quite tricky. We took the gamble on our dry setup from Mallory, hoping that it would come to as the session went on. It certainly took a few laps, but eventually I started settling into the car and getting down to business. The other added complication here was without a doubt me. I'm still yet to put much time in the in the damp conditions, only driving in the dry or the sodden wet at Cadwell and Croft, never the in-between conditions we were facing here today, so for me it was a big learning curve trying to work out where there was grip and where there most definitely wasn't. I was able to finish the session without spinning or putting the car in the gravel, which a large amount of people between the Ma7das and Sports Specials couldn't say, but as I pulled back into the pits, I was very annoyed with myself knowing there was still masses of time left out there. I knew that my lack of experience in the wet was always going to be the biggest issue at a meeting like this, but you have to start somewhere. No matter though, hopefully the track would dry out for the first race and we would have some better luck.

When I got back to the paddock, we had a little debrief on the session and the conditions and I explained that I knew I could have done better. The team were all there for me saying that almost everyone was falling off, locking, or sliding here, there and everywhere, which certainly made me feel a bit better in myself, but there was still a lot of room for improvement. I've never claimed to be particularly good in qualifying this year, so hopefully I could make up for it in the races. The results eventually came and we had qualified 15th for the first race, and 13th for the second. Given the circuit is new to me in conditions I'm not particularly adept in, and that the track is so long you only get about 6 flying laps in, I was more than happy to take that looking back at the grand scheme of things. After checking over the car and a quick drink, it wasn't long before the helmet was going back on ready for the first race.

I sat on the grid ready for the race. Looking out the side of the car at the state of the track – drying but clearly still fairly damp. We'd opted to gamble once again with our fast, dry setup. Proving it at Mallory, I knew if the conditions would come to us, that this setup was going to fly, so we thought there was nothing really to be lost as we were this far back. Because the two races are being held together this weekend, the Sports Specials are starting much further up the grid (as they are the "faster" cars than ours) and beginning their race with the lights (as normal). For us however, to avoid confusion with the initial starters, we would start on the waving of the Union Flag. Now my eyesight is pretty good, so I shan't be complaining here, but my god was it hard to see that guy at the end of the straight waiving that tiny little flag! No matter, the flag dropped (a lot less than the 10 seconds we were told we would be starting behind the Sports Specials might I add, good thing I was paying attention!) and the race got underway. Given the damp conditions, I actually got a cracking shot off the line, advancing myself straight onto the bumper of Imran Khan in front of me. Tentatively through the first corner before hammering it into Maggots and Beckets – a terrific section of track if I do say so myself! As we headed into the corner, I could see Jonathan Lisseter – 2023 Champion – driving slowly and pulling off the track! As it turned out, it was a 50p fuse blowing that ended his race, such a shame for him after a mightily impressive year he's had. The rest of the first lap, and the couple that followed, were rampant with cars dropping off the track, causing countless yellow flags. Add this with having to work my way around the spinning cars made it very tricky keeping up with the cars in front. By about the halfway point of the race, I was an easy 10 car lengths behind a gaggle of about 5 Ma7das, all chopping and changing for position. I got my head down and tried my best to catch up to them, and it was at this point where the race flipped on its head for us. As if by magic, the track was starting to dry out just enough that our gamble of the harder, dry setup was starting to show its form and it wasn't long before I caught the pack up and started getting involved in the action. With only a couple of laps to go, two of the cars in our pack had unfortunately span off and it was down to myself, Imran, and Daniel Cort for what would turn out to be 8th place. At this point, given how many people had fallen off the track, I had no clue what position we were fighting for, but I could taste a couple more places, and I was not going to let them go without a fight.

As we passed the GP pit lane with about a lap and a half to go, Daniel and Imran were battling hard, but slightly compromised themselves through Village and onto the Wellington Straight. I saw my opportunity and set myself up to get a good drive onto the straight, made it past Daniel before pulling out of Aintree and sat on Imran's bumper heading down the straight before pulling out just before the braking zone for Brooklands. Daniel had managed to collect himself and followed me as I moved in on Imran, and pulled the same move I was pulling back on me – three-wide heading into the penultimate corner, with me sandwiched in the middle. Unfortunately, Imran got a big kick of oversteer trying to get into the next corner, leaving just myself and Daniel, side by side through Luffield. I just managed to tip-toe my car onto the power on the slippery inside line and pull onto the start finish straight just in front of him – at this point begging and pleading that I was going to be greeted with the chequered flag.

Pulling through Woodcote and proving that Murphy's Law always prevails, the last lap board was now being held out – all that effort making it into this position and I still needed to hold off these two intense opponents for another lap, God help me! I recall heading into turn one thinking "don't overcook it, don't overcook it, don't overcook it", before promptly overcooking it and pulling a very prominent four-wheel drift through the corner with Daniel and Imran hot on my heels. Managing to collect myself and get through Maggots, Beckets and Chapel sufficiently well, this was now going to be the first chance to lose it, heading down the Hangar straight. I wasn't able to see where Daniel was, but Imran managed to squeeze past me, picking up a cracking tow, and down the inside heading into Stowe. Gluing my car onto his rear bumper, we flew down to the chicane at Vale and he just slightly overcooked it on the brakes in the damp conditions, and I was able to slide through and back in front. Gingerly on the throttle out of the corner and onto Hamilton Straight I was able to get a good run through Abbey and Farm and pull and very marginal break to the cars behind as we headed back onto the Wellington Straight. Unfortunately for them, a little too far back, my pursuers were unable to maximise the tow into the final complex, and I pulled onto the start/finish straight still in

8th place! I vividly recall screaming at the top of my lungs as I pulled through the first few corners on the cooldown lap as I could not believe I had done it! Daniel pulled up alongside me heading into Maggots to give me a thumbs up, which I of course reciprocated for what was a truly stunning end to the race. By the time I made it back to the paddock my voice was starting to go hoarse, but the team were right there to give me a pat on the back for some very impressive racing and a very brave move in some far-from-ideal conditions. Shortly after, I made my way to the garages to shake hands with Imran and Daniel for a thoroughly entertaining race.

"Same again in a couple of hours?"

There were a few hours between the first and second races. The car had proven that once the track starts to dry out just that little bit, that our dry setup was clearly very good after all. It rained for about an hour at the end of our first race, but was then sunny for the rest of the day leading up to our second – surely with all the racing going on today the track would dry up sufficiently to stick with our dry setup again?

Once again, sat on the grid, checking the gauges, waiting for the start of the race. I glanced down at the track, but whereas in the first race I saw a damp but drying piece of tarmac beneath me, this time I saw a dark, glistening ribbon of road, indicating one thing very, very clearly – it was not going to dry! I sat there waiting for the flag to drop thinking in the back of my head how this is not the right setup after all….better hold on tight!

Union flag drops, clutch disengaged, hit the throttle – let's go racing! Straight away greeted by a big kick of oversteer off the line, we head off into the first corner. Spray being kickup all around me and the sun sitting just a little too low as we head into Maggots. There are cars twitching and squirming all around me, and I am not much different! The dry setup that we had opted for is very loose, meaning that when it's dry, you can chuck the car into a corner and dance it through the curve, right on the edge of grip, and keeping tyre scrub to a minimum. As I have proven already in this chapter, this setup just doesn't work when the track is wet. We head through the first corners of the lap and almost every time I gently try to squeeze the throttle on, the back end steps out and I'm forced to fight it with rigorous handfuls of opposite-lock. Everyone is clearly struggling in the conditions, but you can easily tell those who are well practiced in these conditions, driving as if the track beneath them is dry! Unfortunately, despite my best efforts, I just wasn't able to keep up with the leaders. I could hold on for a couple of corners, but it wouldn't take them long to pull away from me.

I continued to do battle with the conditions for the rest of the race, with only one pirouette at the final corner, a couple of laps from the end. Eventually the chequered flag flew for the final time of the year and we scored 16th place.

Upon returning back to the paddock, I switched the car off, jumped out and celebrated the result with the team. Although not a particularly impressive final race position, this result banked exactly what we needed.

With Dave Mason and Martin West had not making it to Silverstone this weekend, and with the scores I had amassed, we were unofficially confirmed as finishing 6th in the championship!

6th in the championship, when two months before the start of the season, I had never driven one of these cars, and didn't even have one myself, I absolutely could not believe it. Astonished at what we had achieved and how far we've come doesn't even begin to express it. However, that wasn't all we were celebrating. Although there was no award for it, we self-declared ourselves as the highest scoring rookie of the year, and just to put the cherry on the cake, we were the only car to finish every race. You know what, I'll take that for a first go!

CHAPTER 24 – "WELL, WHAT NOW THEN…"

Date: 02/11/2023

Time: 08:11

Location: Work

Ping (Message from Dad)

Dad: "I'm worried we've not had any stupid ideas recently"

ACKNOWLEDGEMENTS

Most people have been sufficiently acknowledged this year as it is (normally in payments of beer!), but I think it would only be just of me to mention them here, because there is no doubt in my mind that all of this just wouldn't be possible without them!

Firstly, I've got to put a massive shoutout to my Dad. Always keen to get stuck into a "stupid idea", he's been with me since day one on this project; chief engineer, race engineer, driver coach, head chef, transportation manager, lead ice cream buyer, you name it! I cannot thank him enough for everything, I just hope he's enjoyed the journey as much as I have.

Then where would I be without my darling fiancée, Bex. For all the late nights down the garage and early mornings I've taken off and left her at home, I think I might have to buy her a fairly kick-ass Christmas present to say thank you! She's been absolutely amazing this year (like she always is to be fair!) and I couldn't do it without her support, so thank you, sweet.

Mum, for all the support and help throughout the year, and for donating so much of dads help over the past 10-months, thank you.

Then onto everyone who's helped throughout the year. Of course, there is Ross and Brian for all the help they've given and all the fibreglassing they've done! Stan, Jordy, Tom, Joe, and Hannah, for giving up your weekends to come and help with the car at the track (and Tom especially for the Tuesday nights down the garage, although the pizza is probably payment enough ☐).

And then of course Alan Coller, Dave Boucher, Stuart Sellars, Ben Powney, David Winter, and David Bowen for all the help and advice they've given over the year! And of course, off the back of that, everyone in the Ma7da Championship. You've all been amazing, and I cannot wait to get back out next year and do it all over again.

Photo credits go to the fantastic Jonathan Elsey Photography, and SJN Photography.

Penultimately, a huge shoutout to Electrified Automation. You may have noticed their logo on the car, but they have been a key cornerstone in getting the car out this year, so a massive thank you to everyone there too.

And finally, thank you to you, the reader. You may have thought that most of this book is bollocks, and you're probably right, but if you've made it this far, then thank you. I've thoroughly enjoyed writing this book, and I hope you've enjoyed it too.

Printed in Great Britain
by Amazon